I WONDER WHY ENCYCLOPEDIA

I WONDER WHY ENCYCLOPEDIA

Kingfisher

KINGFISHER
An imprint of Larousse plc
Elsley House, 24–30 Great Titchfield Street
London W1P 7AD

Material in this edition previously published by Kingfisher
in the *I Wonder Why* series.

This edition first published by Kingfisher 1996
10 9 8 7 6 5 4 3 2
This edition copyright © Larousse plc 1996

ISBN 0 7534 0108 8

Printed in FRANCE

Project editor: Clare Oliver
Contributing editors: Brigid Avison, Jackie Gaff,
Claire Llewellyn
Editorial assistant: Virginie Verhague

Cover design: Smiljka Surla
I Wonder Why **series designer:** David West Children's Books
Additional design: Smiljka Surla
Art editor: Christina Fraser
Picture referencing: Amanda Francis

Publishing director: Jim Miles

Production manager: Susan Latham

Contributing authors: Brigid Avison; Andrew Charman;
Anita Ganeri; Christopher Maynard; Richard Mead; Clare
Oliver; Amanda O'Neill; Josephine Paker; Steve Parker; Philip
Steele; Carole Stott; Barbara Taylor; Rod
Theodorou; Brenda Walpole; Jenny Wood

Contributing consultants: Andrew Branson;
British Museum: Department of
Egyptian Antiquities and
Department of Graeco-Roman
Antiquites; Michael Chinery;
Eryl Davies; Dougal Dixon; Ian
Graham; David Haycock, Paul Hillyard;
Dr David Hughes; Keith Lye; Dr
Elizabeth McCall Smith; Geoff Puplett;
Dr Peter Rowan; Peter Thoms

CONTENTS

THE UNIVERSE AND PLANET EARTH

The Universe
14 What is the universe?
14 When did it begin?
15 Will the universe ever end?
16 What is the Milky Way?
17 How many stars are there?
18 What are stars made of?
19 Why do stars twinkle?
19 Are stars star-shaped?
20 What is a red giant?
21 Which stars explode?

Our solar system
22 How hot is the Sun?
23 Will the Sun ever go out?
24 How many planets are there?
25 What's the difference between stars and planets?
26 Which is the hottest planet?
27 Which is the red planet?
28 Which is the biggest planet?
30 Which planet is farthest from the Sun?
30 Which is the coldest planet?
31 How do we know about the farthest planets?

Planet Earth
32 Is the Earth round?
33 What is the Earth made of?
34 How old is the Earth?
35 Has the Earth changed much?

Mountains, volcanoes and earthquakes
36 Where are the highest mountains?
37 Can mountains shrink?
38 Which mountains breathe fire?
39 Do people live on volcanoes?
40 What makes the Earth shake?
41 Can people tell if an earthquake is coming?

The sky and the weather
42 How high is the sky?
42 What is the greenhouse effect?
44 What are clouds made of?
44 When does rain fall from clouds?
45 How cold is snow?
46 Where do thunderstorms start?
47 What is thunder?
48 What is a tornado?
49 Why does the wind blow?

Oceans
50 How big is the ocean?
51 Which is the biggest ocean?
51 What's the difference between a sea and an ocean?
52 What makes waves roll?

SCIENCE AND THE HUMAN BODY

■ PART 1: SCIENCE
54 What is science about?
55 What do scientists do?

Energy and heat
56 Why do I run out of energy?
57 What is energy?
58 Why does the spoon get hot when I stir my cocoa?
58 Why is sunlight warm?
59 How do hang-gliders hitch lifts?

Sound

60   What is sound?
61   Why do trumpeters blow raspberries?
61   Can sound travel under water?

Air, light and water

62   What is air made of?
63   How do bubbles get into fizzy drinks?
63   Why do cakes rise?
64   Why do shadows happen?
65   Why can I see through glass?
66   Can light bounce?
67   Why do my legs look shorter under water?
68   Why do rainbows happen?
69   Why is grass green?
69   Can cats see in colour?
70   What can walk on water?
70   Why are water droplets round?
71   Why does soap make bubbles?
72   Why do we need air?
72   Why do we need light?
73   Why do we need water?

■ PART 2: HUMAN BODY

Being born

74   Where do I come from?
75   What is my tummy button?

Bones

76   How many bones do I have?
77   What is my funny bone?

Muscles and blood

78   How do I move?
78   Why do strong people have big muscles?
79   What is cramp?
80   What does my heart do?
81   What is blood for?
81   How big is my heart?

My head: inside and out

82   What is inside my head?
83   What makes me feel things?
84   Why do I breathe?
85   What makes me hiccup?
85   What makes me sneeze?
86   Why do I blink?
87   Why can't I see in the dark?
88   Why are ears such a funny shape?
88   Why do I feel dizzy when I spin around?
90   What is my nose for?
91   What is my tongue for?
91   Why do teeth fall out?

Illness

92   Why do I get ill sometimes?

TRANSPORT AND BUILDINGS

■ PART 1: TRANSPORT

Speed

94   How far can I go in an hour?
96   Which is the fastest car?
96   Which is the fastest boat?
97   Which is the fastest plane?

In the air

98   Which plane can waggle its nose?
99   Can planes move their wings?
100   Do airships run on air?
101   Why do hot-air balloons float?

On land

102   Why do cars have wheels?
103   Which are the biggest tyres?
103   Which ships have wheels?
104   Why do cars need petrol?
105   What happens inside car engines?
106   Do road trains run on rails?
107   Can trains fly?

By water
108 Why don't ships sink?
108 How do submarines sink?
109 Which ships fly?

Transporting transport
110 Which plane rides piggyback?
111 When do cars hitch rides?

■ PART 2: BUILDING

Houses
112 What are houses made from?
114 What holds up the ceiling?
115 What's behind the walls?
115 What's under the floor?

Building
116 Why do houses need holes?
117 What do diggers do?
118 Do buildings have roots?
118 Which are the world's biggest hammers?
119 Which are the world's largest corkscrews?
120 Do buildings have a skeleton?
120 Do buildings have a skin?

Knocking buildings down
122 Why are some buildings knocked down?
122 How do you wreck a building?
123 How do you clear up all the mess?

Landmarks
124 Which are the world's tallest buildings?
125 When was the first skyscraper built?
126 Which roof opens when the Sun shines?
126 Which building is inside out?

Tunnels and bridges
128 Why are tunnels round?
129 How do you tunnel through hard rock?
129 Can a mole dig as fast as a TBM?
130 How are bridges built?
131 Do bridges sway about in the wind?
132 Which bridge can break in two?

■ INVENTIONS:

134 Why do people invent things?
135 Is everything invented?
135 Where do inventors get their ideas?

Measuring time
136 Which calendar was carved in stone?
136 Who invented our calendar?
137 What is a leap year?
137 Why do we need calendars?
138 Why does my watch tick?
138 How did people manage before clocks?
139 How does a grandfather keep good time?
140 How can you split a second?
140 Which timer was a load of old rope?
141 How can you cook an egg with sand?

Money
142 How did a till settle a row?
143 Who used tea as money?
143 How can a supermarket trolley make you rich?

Home and garden

144 What did people use before fridges?
144 Who ate the first cornflakes?
145 How were drinking straws invented?
146 How do you make toast without a toaster?
147 Who invented the microwave oven?
147 Why don't non-stick frying pans stick?
148 Who first flushed the toilet?
149 Who first jumped in the bath?
149 How did horses help keep carpets clean?
150 Which came first – screws or screwdrivers?
150 Who had everything under lock and key?
151 Could a horse mow the lawn?

Health and beauty

152 Which new invention was soon on everyone's lips?
152 Who wore a mouthful of hippo teeth?
153 Why were plasters first invented?
154 Who invented raincoats?
154 Why do zips have teeth?
155 Can clothes keep you feeling fit?

Sport and games

156 Who scored goals in a basket?
156 Why are trainers so springy?
157 How did people ice-skate in summer?
158 Why are bears called teddies?
159 Which toy is 6,000 years old?
159 When did home computer games appear?

Transport

160 What were the first cars like?
160 How do you ride on air?
161 Which bikes have sails?
162 Who cycled over the sea?
162 Can bikes climb mountains?
163 How many people can ride on a bike?

Communication

164 How can you fit 1,000 books in your pocket?
165 Which computer was as big as a bus?
165 Who was Mr Biro?
166 Who took hours to take a photo?
166 When could you watch pink TV?
167 Who invented the personal stereo?
168 Why does the telephone ring?
169 How can glass link the world?
169 Are phone lines just for voices?
170 Can a robot play the piano?
171 Where do people mix music?
171 Can you be an entire orchestra?
172 How can you fight a hungry dinosaur?

HISTORY

Prehistory

174 How long ago did dinosaurs live?
175 How many dinosaurs were there?
176 How are dinosaur fossils found?
177 Where are dinosaurs found?
178 What happened to the dinosaurs?
179 Are there any dinosaurs around today?

The Ancient World

180 Why do we call Egyptians ancient?
181 Why were the Egyptians great?
182 Who ruled Egypt?
183 Could a woman be pharoah?
183 How would you know if you met a pharoah?
184 Why did the Egyptians bury their mummies?
185 Why were mummies brainless?
185 Why were mummies wrapped in bandages?
186 Why were the pyramids built?
188 Who were the Ancient Greeks?
189 How did Greece grow bigger and bigger?

190 Who was the goddess of wisdom?
191 Who told stories about the gods?
192 Who were the Romans?
193 Did all the Romans live in Rome?
194 Where can you visit Ancient Rome?
195 How do we know about the Romans?

The Middle Ages
196 What were the Middle Ages
     in the middle of?
198 Why did castles have moats?
200 Why did knights
     wear armour?
202 Where was Vinland
     the Good?
203 Who went to sea in junks?
203 Was Sinbad a real sailor?
204 Where did Robin Hood
     live?
205 Who was Joan of Arc?
205 Who was a teenage
warrior?

Recent times
206 Who were the Tudors?
207 What happened to
the Aztecs?
208 Who made a new home in the
     New World?
209 Who built the best home for the
     next world?
210 Who was the 'last' king of France?
211 Who was the first president of the
     United States?
212 Who steamed into the twentieth
     century?

COUNTRIES AND PEOPLES

Around the world
214 What is a country?
215 Why do countries fly
     flags?
216 How many countries
     are there?

218 Which country has the most people?
219 Which is the biggest country?
219 Where is there land but no countries?
220 Where are there only two seasons?
221 Where does it pour for a month?

Cities
222 Which city is above the clouds?
223 Why do Venetians walk on water?
223 Which is the world's biggest city?

Transport
224 Who rides on a snowmobile?
225 Where do you park your bike in
     China?
225 Who paints pictures on trucks?

Language
226 Who writes with a paintbrush?
226 Who reads back-to-front?
227 Which country speaks over
     800 languages?

Food and farming
228 Which is the oldest dish on the menu?
229 Who eats shells, butterflies
     and little worms?
229 Where does it take all afternoon
     to have a cup of tea?
230 Where are wheatfields bigger
     than countries?
231 Where does chocolate grow on trees?
231 Which country has more sheep
     than people?

Clothes and customs
232 Where do women wear bowler hats?
232 Where do men wear skirts?
233 Which dress has no stitches?
234 Who wears bank-notes at their
     wedding?
235 Where are children made
     kings and queens?
235 Who sticks out their
     tongue at strangers?
236 Who lights the lamps
     at New Year?

236 Who brings in the New Year
    with a bang?
237 Who blows a horn at New Year?
238 Where do elephants glow in the dark?
238 When do people eat green food?
239 When is the Day of the Dead?

Entertainment
240 Where can you play an oil drum?
240 Who bangs on the bongos?
241 Can drums talk?
242 Where can you find a gamelan?
243 Are rattles just for babies?
243 What roars like a bull?
244 How do termites help to make music?
244 Which harp fits inside your mouth?
245 Which instrument is made with a
    spider's web?
246 Where do children watch shadows?
247 Who makes pictures from sand?
247 Which dancers snap their fingers?
248 Why do people race camels?
249 Which is the world's most
    popular sport?

Homes
250 Who lives in a longhouse?
251 Where do gardens grow on rivers?
251 How do you keep cosy in the Gobi?
252 Could people live in space?

ANIMALS VOLUME I

Kinds of animal
255 Which is the biggest animal?
256 What's the difference between
    sharks and dolphins?
258 What's the difference
    between frogs and
    toads?
258 …and alligators and
    crocodiles?
259 …and between
    monkeys and apes?
259 …and rabbits and hares?

260 Why do animals have
    skeletons inside their bodies?
261 Which animals have skeletons
    on the outside?

Animal conservation
262 When do animals like going
    to the zoo?
262 When do animals like leaving the zoo?
263 Which endangered animal is brought
    up in a bucket?
264 Why do animals need us?
265 Why do we need animals?

Land animals
266 What's it like at the poles?
266 Which is the coldest place
    in the world?
267 Where do polar bears live?
268 Why do camels have humps?
268 Why do elephants have trunks?
269 Why do giraffes have long necks?
270 How high can a kangaroo hop?
270 How fast can a cheetah run?
271 Which animal has an extra hand?
272 How many ants can an anteater eat?
273 Which animal uses its finger as a fork?
273 Which is the greediest animal?
274 When does a puppy grow into a dog?
275 When does a tiger cub leave home?
276 Which animal is always
    being washed?
277 Who enjoys a good groom?
277 Which animal lives in the
    cleanest nest?

Reptiles
278 Do snakes have good table manners?
279 Why do snakes have teeth and fangs?
279 Why do snakes stare?
280 Which lizard looks both ways at once?
280 Why does a snake flick its tongue?
281 What use is a hole in the head?
282 Whose tongue is longer than its tail?
282 Why do lizards lose their tails?
283 Why do geckos lick their eyes?

283 Are there still dragons on Earth?
284 Which reptile has a frightful frill?
284 Which turtle kicks up a stink?
285 Why do some snakes pretend
     to be dead?
286 Which reptile is a living fortress?
286 Do turtles have teeth?
287 Which turtle breathes through
     a snorkel?
288 Do reptiles have skin like ours?
289 Why do snakes shed their skin?
289 Why do some lizards have
     horns and spikes?

Birds
290 Why do birds have feathers?
290 Which bird can fly backwards?
291 Why can't penguins fly?
292 What's inside a bird's egg?

ANIMALS VOLUME II

Creepy-crawlies
294 Which is the biggest creepy-crawly?
295 Which is the smallest creepy-crawly?
296 What is an insect?
296 When is a fly not a fly?
297 What is a bug?
297 Are spiders insects?
298 Why do spiders spin webs?
298 How do spiders make thread?
299 When do spiders fly?
300 What does an insect feel
     with its feelers?
301 Which insect tastes with its toes?
301 Which insect listens with its legs?
302 Why do caterpillars change into
     butterflies?
304 Which insects wear armour?
304 Which beetle fires a spray gun?
305 What digs graves, then robs them?
306 Which insect makes the best mother?
306 What hatches out in a vase?
307 Which insect is the laziest parent?
308 When is a flower not a flower?

309 When is a leaf not a leaf?
309 Which insect has a
     fierce bottom?
310 Why do bees live in hives?
310 Why do bees dance?
311 Why do bees carry brushes
     and baskets?
312 Which ants live in a tent?
312 Whose house has a trapdoor?
313 Whose nest is paper thin?
314 What has a sting in its tail?
314 Can spiders kill people?
315 What kills over a million people a
     year?
315 Which killing machine has 120 million
     legs?
316 Are creepy-crawlies good for people?
317 Are people good for creepy-crawlies?

Water animals
318 Which is the biggest fish?
318 Which is the fastest fish?
319 Which is the biggest crab?
320 How do fish breathe under water?
320 How do fish swim?
321 Which bird flies under water?
321 Which animal is jet-propelled?
322 Which fish has headlights?
322 How deep is the ocean?
323 Are there worms
     under the sea?
324 Where do angels,
     clowns and parrots live?
325 What is a coral reef?
325 Where is the biggest reef?
326 Which fish hunts with a hammer?
326 Which is the most shocking fish?
327 Which fish look like stones?
328 Which animals shoot their food?

329 **INDEX**

THE UNIVERSE AND THE EARTH

What is the universe?

The whole world and everything beyond it is the universe. It is all the stars and planets, the Earth and its plants and animals, you and me – everything.

- You are made of the same stuff as a star!

- There are huge groups of stars in space. They're called galaxies, and they're like gigantic star-cities.

- The Big Bang explosion sent the young universe flying out in all directions. Over vast ages of time, bits came together to make galaxies.

- The galaxies are still speeding apart today, and the universe is getting bigger.

When did it begin?

- To see how the universe is getting bigger, watch the spots as you blow up a spotty balloon.

Many astronomers think that everything in the universe was once packed together in one small lump. Then, about 15 billion years ago, there was a gigantic explosion which they call the Big Bang.

Will the universe ever end?

Some astronomers think the universe will just carry on getting bigger as the galaxies speed apart. Others think that the galaxies may one day start falling back towards each other until they crash together in a Big Crunch!

● Astronomers are scientists who study the stars and the planets.

● No one knows where all the material to make the universe came from in the first place.

What is the Milky Way?

The Milky Way is the galaxy we live in. It is made up of all the stars you can see in the sky at night, and lots and lots more you can't see.

● The Milky Way is a spiral galaxy. Below you can see what it looks like from above – a bit like a whirlpool with long spiralling arms.

● From the side, a spiral galaxy looks like two fried eggs stuck together.

● The Milky Way got its name because at night we can sometimes see part of it looking like a band of milky white light across the sky.

● We live on a planet called Earth, which travels around a star called the Sun.

16

● Astronomers usually give galaxies numbers instead of names. Only a few have names that tell us what they look like – the Whirlpool, the Sombrero, and the Black Eye, for example!

● These are the three main galaxy shapes.

Irregular (no special shape)

Elliptical (egg-shaped)

Spiral

How many stars are there?

There are about 1000 billion stars in the Milky Way. That's nearly 200 stars for every person living on Earth today!

Although we can't see all of it, astronomers have worked out how big the universe is and how many stars it has. There are about 100 billion billion stars, in around 100 billion galaxies. It's hard even to think about so many stars, let alone count them!

17

What are stars made of?

Stars aren't solid like the ground beneath your feet. Instead, they are made of gases like the air around you.

The two main gases in stars are called hydrogen and helium. They are the stars' fuel. Stars make heat and light from them.

● Sometimes huge flame-like sheets of glowing gas shoot out from a star. These are called prominences.

● Since earliest times, people have seen patterns in the way stars are grouped in the sky. The patterns are called constellations.

● The brightest star we can see in the night sky is called Sirius. Another name for it is the Dog Star. It is about twice as big as our Sun, but it gives out more than twenty times as much light!

Why do stars twinkle?

Stars only twinkle when we look at them from Earth. Out in space their light shines steadily. We see them twinkling and shimmering because of the air around the Earth – as light from a star travels towards us, it is bent and wobbled by bubbles of hot and cold air.

● Light bends when it passes through different things. If you put a straw in a glass of water, for example, it looks bent because it is half in air and half in water.

Are stars star-shaped?

No, stars are round, like balls. We give them pointy edges when we draw them because this is what they look like from Earth, with their light blinking and twinkling.

What is a red giant?

All stars are born, live for a very long time and then die. A red giant is a huge old star.

● Stars are being born all the time. They start their lives in star-nurseries called clusters.

3 Most stars are like our Sun and shine steadily for nearly all their lives.

2 The gas and dust come together to make lots of balls, which become star clusters.

1 All stars are born in huge spinning clouds of gas and dust. Our Sun was born 4.6 billion years ago.

● If you think of our Sun as shining like a car's headlights, then a red giant would shine like a lighthouse!

4 Towards the end of their lives, stars like our Sun swell up and become as much as 100 times bigger. They turn into red giants. Our Sun will do this in about 5 billion years' time.

● On Earth, a sugar-lump-sized piece of a white dwarf would weigh as much as a small car!

5 When it has used up all its gas fuel, a red giant shrinks down into a white dwarf. It is then about 10,000 times smaller, but still very hot.

6 The star cools down and ends its life billions of years later, as a black dwarf – a cold black cinder.

● Stars must have at least eight times as much gas fuel as our Sun to end their lives in supernova explosions.

Which stars explode?

Different sorts of star lead different lives. Some stars have a lot more gas fuel in them than others. These really massive stars don't die quietly, by cooling down. Instead, they blow up in a great flash of light. Stars that explode like this are called supernovas.

How hot is the Sun?

Like all stars, our Sun is a huge ball of super-hot gas. It is hottest in the middle – the temperature there is around 15 million ˚C.

The outside of the Sun is a lot cooler than the middle – only 6000 ˚C. But this is still 25 times hotter than the hottest kitchen oven!

● Dark patches called sunspots come and go on the face of the Sun. They make it look as though it has chickenpox. Sunspots are dark because they are cooler and so give out less light than the rest of the Sun.

● Most sunspots are larger than the Earth.

● Plants and animals couldn't live without the Sun's heat and light.

● The Sun is the only star that's close enough to Earth for us to feel its heat. The next nearest star to Earth is called Proxima Centauri. Our Sun's light takes 8.3 minutes to reach us, but Proxima Centauri's takes 4.3 years!

● The Sun uses more than 30 million truck loads of fuel every second!

Will the Sun ever go out?

One day the Sun will use up all its gas fuel and die. But this won't happen in your lifetime, or your children's, or even your great-great-great grandchildren's! Astronomers think that the Sun has enough gas fuel to last for at least another 5 billion years.

How many planets are there?

Our planet, the Earth, has eight neighbours. Together they make a family of nine planets which travel around the Sun. We call the Sun, and all the space bodies that whirl around it, the solar system.

Besides the Sun and the planets, the solar system includes moons, mini-planets called asteroids, and comets.

● The word planet comes from the Greek word *planetes*, which means wanderer.

● Comets are rather like huge dirty snowballs. Most stay out on the edge of the solar system, but a few travel close to the Sun. These comets grow gas and dust tails, millions of kilometres long, when the Sun's heat starts to melt them.

Mercury Venus Earth Mars Jupiter

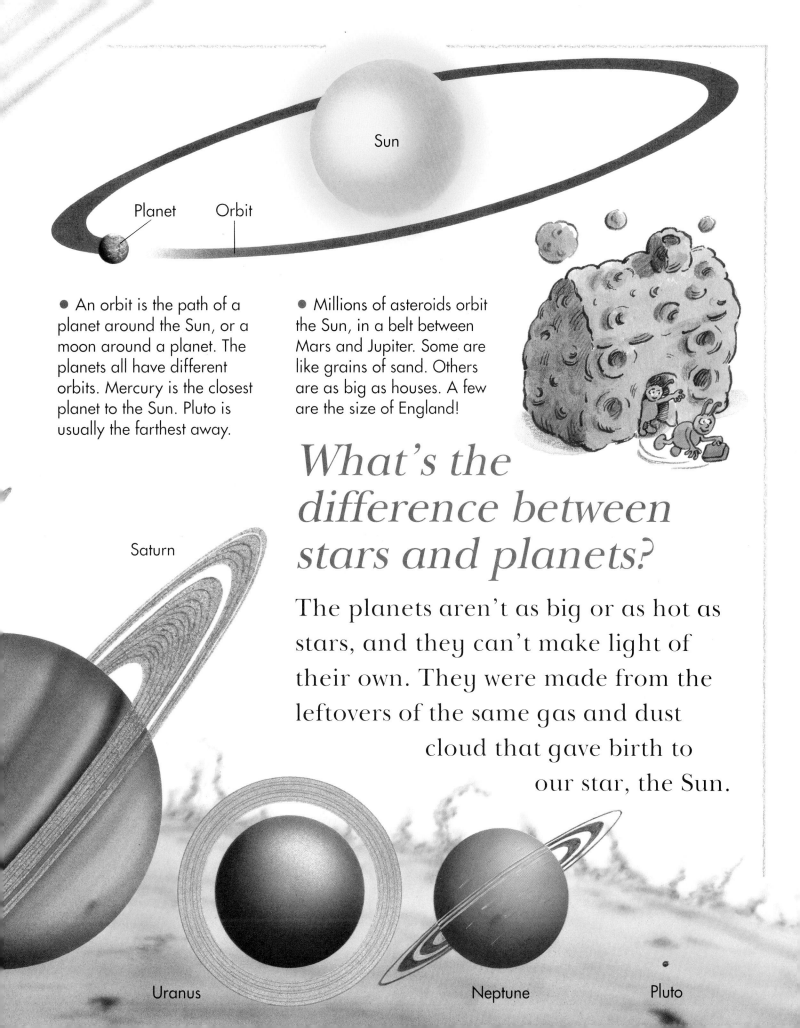

Sun

Planet Orbit

● An orbit is the path of a planet around the Sun, or a moon around a planet. The planets all have different orbits. Mercury is the closest planet to the Sun. Pluto is usually the farthest away.

● Millions of asteroids orbit the Sun, in a belt between Mars and Jupiter. Some are like grains of sand. Others are as big as houses. A few are the size of England!

What's the difference between stars and planets?

The planets aren't as big or as hot as stars, and they can't make light of their own. They were made from the leftovers of the same gas and dust cloud that gave birth to our star, the Sun.

Saturn

Uranus

Neptune

Pluto

Which is the hottest planet?

Venus isn't the closest planet to the Sun, but it is the hottest. The temperature there can reach 500 °C – that's about eight times hotter than it gets in the Sahara Desert, the hottest place on Earth.

● Although Mercury (right) is closer to the Sun, Venus is hotter! This is because Venus is covered by clouds of gas which act like a blanket, keeping in the Sun's heat.

● Space probes have landed on Venus and sent back pictures and information to Earth. The probes were destroyed soon after landing, however, by the terrible climate on Venus.

● Mars is the next planet after ours from the Sun, and people once thought that like Earth it might have living things. Space probes were sent, but they didn't find any signs of life!

Which is the red planet?

Mars is often called the red planet. The ground there is covered in dusty red soil, which gets swept up by the wind to make pink clouds! The rocks on Mars have lots of iron in them, and iron goes red when it rusts. A better name for Mars might be the rusty planet!

● Mercury is covered in craters – hollows made by huge space rocks crashing into it.

● If you could visit Mercury, you would see that the Sun looks more than twice as big there as it does from Earth. This is because Mercury is so much closer to the Sun.

● Living things need water. If there is any on Mars, it is frozen inside its north and south polar ice caps.

Which is the biggest planet?

Jupiter is so huge that all the other planets could fit inside it! The beautiful patterns on its face are made by swirling clouds of gas, stirred up by powerful wind storms.

● Jupiter's Great Red Spot is so big that two Earths could fit inside it! It is a gigantic storm which has been raging for over 300 years.

● Jupiter was named by the Ancient Romans, after the king of their gods.

● Jupiter is one of four planets with rings around them.

Great Red Spot

● The planets Jupiter, Saturn, Uranus and Neptune are called the gas giants. They are all very big, and they are all mainly made of gas, with small rocky centres.

Saturn's rings

● Many people think Saturn's glistening rings make it the most beautiful planet in the solar system. Pictures sent back to Earth by space probes have shown us that the rings are made up of ice, rock and dust.

● Astronomers send telescopes into space, because the air around the Earth stops some of the light and other information from stars and planets from reaching us. The Hubble Space Telescope was launched in 1990. It can see nearly to the edge of the universe!

Hubble Space Telescope

Which planet is farthest from the Sun?

Although for most of the time Pluto is the most distant planet, every 248 years its orbit brings it closer to the Sun than Neptune!

● Between 1979 and 1999, Pluto's orbit makes Neptune farthest from the Sun.

Pluto **3**

3

Sun

1

2

Uranus **1**

Neptune **2**

● One of the gases in Uranus is called methane. It gives the planet its bluey-green colour.

Which is the coldest planet?

Ice-cream would taste as hot as soup on Pluto, where the temperature is an unbelievably icy -240 °C! Pluto is so cold because it is very far from the Sun. It is almost 40 times farther away than Earth is.

How do we know about the farthest planets?

Until the American Voyager 2 space probe visited Uranus in 1986 and Neptune in 1989, not a lot was known about these two planets. They are too far away for us to see them clearly from Earth, even through the most powerful telescopes.

Voyager 2's cameras showed that Neptune has eight moons. Earth-based astronomers could only see two using telescopes.

● Voyager 2 left Earth in 1977 and reached Neptune twelve years later, in 1989.

Is the Earth round?

If you were an astronaut floating about in space, the Earth would look like a gigantic ball. It isn't perfectly round, though. Like a ball that's been gently squashed, it's slightly flatter at the top and bottom, and it bulges out just a little at the middle.

Equator

● The Earth measures 40,075 kilometres around its 'waist' – the equator. If you walked night and day, it would take you more than a year to get this far!

● The Earth looks blue from space. That's because nearly three-quarters of it is covered by the sea.

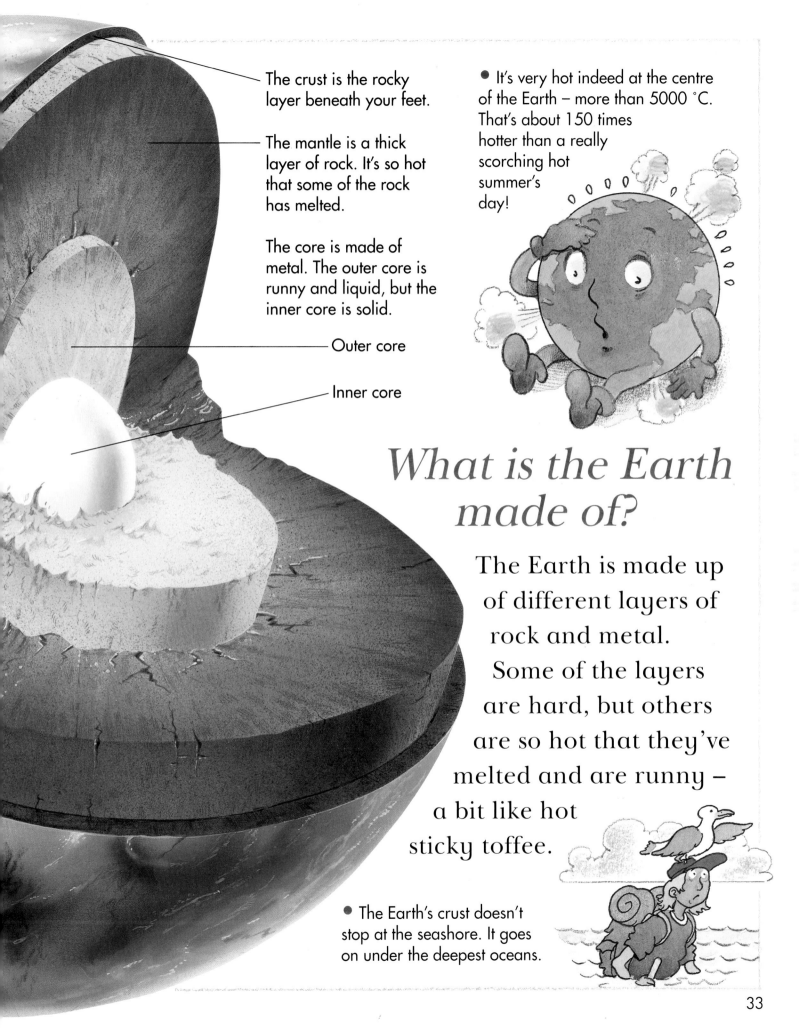

The crust is the rocky layer beneath your feet.

The mantle is a thick layer of rock. It's so hot that some of the rock has melted.

The core is made of metal. The outer core is runny and liquid, but the inner core is solid.

Outer core

Inner core

● It's very hot indeed at the centre of the Earth – more than 5000 °C. That's about 150 times hotter than a really scorching hot summer's day!

What is the Earth made of?

The Earth is made up of different layers of rock and metal. Some of the layers are hard, but others are so hot that they've melted and are runny – a bit like hot sticky toffee.

● The Earth's crust doesn't stop at the seashore. It goes on under the deepest oceans.

How old is the Earth?

Scientists think the Earth formed about 4,600 million years ago – although no one was there to see! They think the Moon formed then, too.

● Human beings are very new to the Earth. If you imagine our planet's 4600-million-year-long history squeezed into one year, people have only been around since late on 31 December!

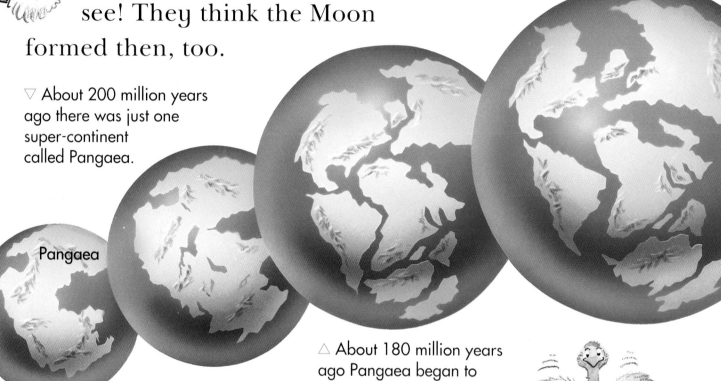

▽ About 200 million years ago there was just one super-continent called Pangaea.

Pangaea

△ About 180 million years ago Pangaea began to break up.

● Continents are massive pieces of land. There are seven of them in all. Trace them from a map, and try to see how they once fitted together.

● Emus live in Australia, rheas in South America, and ostriches in Africa. They look similar, and none of them can fly. They may have been related to one kind of bird. It could have walked to all three continents millions of years ago, when the land was joined.

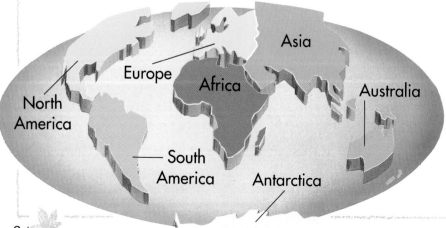

North America
Europe
Asia
Africa
Australia
South America
Antarctica

Has the Earth changed much?

Yes, it has! About 300 million years ago, most of the land was joined together in one big piece. Then it began to break up into smaller pieces called continents. These slowly drifted apart, until they reached the places they're in today.

▽ About 65 million years ago the continents drifted farther apart.

▽ Today, the continents are still drifting.

● North America and Europe are still moving apart by about 4 centimetres each year. That's about the length of your thumb.

Where are the highest mountains?

The Himalayas in Asia are the world's highest mountains. They're so high that they're known as 'the roof of the world'. The towering mountain peaks are bitterly cold places, where the snow and ice never melt.

● Himalaya means 'home of the snows'. It's a good name for these freezing peaks.

● These are the highest mountains in each continent:

Asia – Mt Everest 8848 m

S. America – Aconcagua 6959 m

N. America – Mt McKinley 6194 m

Africa – Mt Kilimanjaro 5895 m

Europe – Mt Elbrus 5633 m

Antarctica – Vinson Massif 5139 m

Australia – Mt Kosciusko 2230 m

Can mountains shrink?

Many mountains are getting smaller all the time. Every day, small chips of rock are carried away by ice, snow and running water.

Some mountains are getting bigger, though. The Himalayas are still being pushed up by movements inside the Earth.

● In Hawaii there is a mountain called Mauna Kea which is more than 1,300 metres higher than Mount Everest. Most of it is under the sea, though.

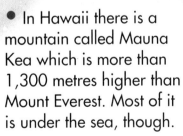

● The higher you go up a mountain, the colder it becomes. Many of the animals that live high up on mountains have thick woolly coats to keep out the cold – goats, llamas and yaks, for example.

Which mountains breathe fire?

Volcanoes are mountains that sometimes spurt out burning ash, gas, and hot runny rock called lava. The gas and fiery lava come from deep down inside the Earth, and burst up through cracks in the crust.

● The saucer-like top of a volcano is called a crater. Sometimes a dead volcano's crater fills with rainwater and makes a beautiful lake.

● There are about 500 active volcanoes on land. There are even more under the sea.

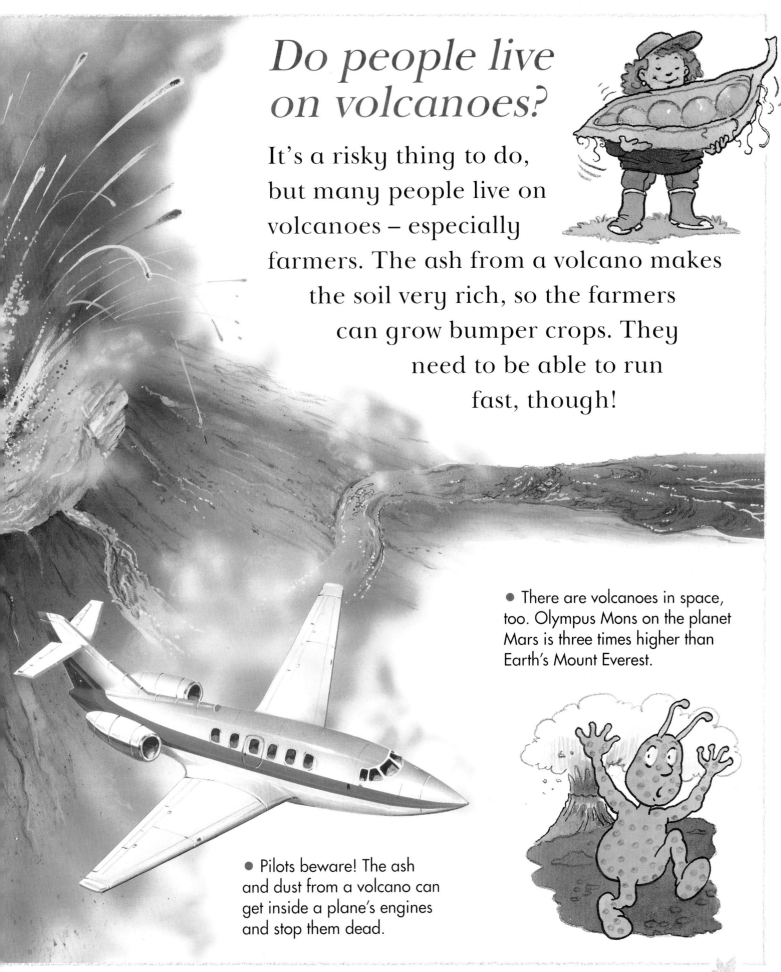

Do people live on volcanoes?

It's a risky thing to do, but many people live on volcanoes – especially farmers. The ash from a volcano makes the soil very rich, so the farmers can grow bumper crops. They need to be able to run fast, though!

● There are volcanoes in space, too. Olympus Mons on the planet Mars is three times higher than Earth's Mount Everest.

● Pilots beware! The ash and dust from a volcano can get inside a plane's engines and stop them dead.

What makes the Earth shake?

The Earth's surface is made up of huge pieces of hard rock which drift on the hot runny rock below. Sometimes these pieces push and shove against each other, making the Earth shake. This is what happens during an earthquake.

● In the worst earthquakes the ground cracks open, streets sink, and buildings crumble to piles of rubble.

● The greatest danger in an earthquake is a building collapsing on top of you. Sheltering under a table or a doorway may save your life.

Can people tell if an earthquake is coming?

Scientists who study earthquakes are called seismologists. Although they know where earthquakes are likely to happen, they usually can't say exactly when.

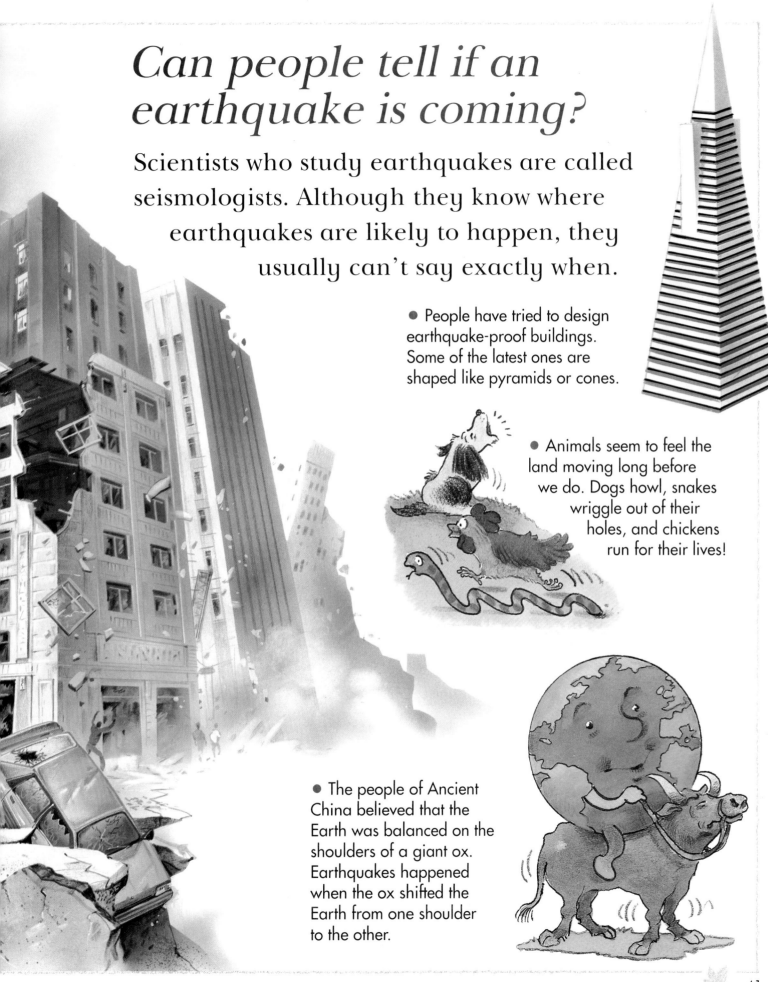

● People have tried to design earthquake-proof buildings. Some of the latest ones are shaped like pyramids or cones.

● Animals seem to feel the land moving long before we do. Dogs howl, snakes wriggle out of their holes, and chickens run for their lives!

● The people of Ancient China believed that the Earth was balanced on the shoulders of a giant ox. Earthquakes happened when the ox shifted the Earth from one shoulder to the other.

How high is the sky?

The sky is part of an invisible skin of air around the Earth. This skin is called the atmosphere, and it reaches out into space for about 500 kilometres.

There's a very important gas called oxygen in the atmosphere – we all need to breathe oxygen to stay alive.

● The Earth is the only planet known to have enough oxygen for living things.

● If the Earth gets too hot, the ice at the Poles could melt. The seas would rise and drown many towns along the coasts.

What is the greenhouse effect?

The greenhouse effect is the name scientists have given to a hot problem. Waste gases from factories, power stations and cars are building up in the atmosphere and trapping too much heat close to the Earth. Our planet is slowly getting warmer – like a greenhouse in summer.

OZONE LAYER

3 Above the planes is the ozone layer. This works a bit like a sunblock, protecting us from the Sun's burning rays.

2 Planes fly in the next layer, high above the clouds where the skies are clear. The air is thinner here, and has less oxygen in it.

1 The atmosphere is made up of different layers. In the lowest layer, the air carries clouds and weather around the Earth.

What are clouds made of?

Some clouds look like they're made of cotton wool – but they're not! Clouds are made of billions of water droplets and ice crystals. These are so tiny and light that they float in the air.

● You'd need your umbrella on Mount Wai-'ale-'ale in Hawaii. It rains there for 350 days each year.

● Without rain, no plants would grow. Then what would we all eat?

When does rain fall from clouds?

Rain falls when water droplets in a cloud start joining together. They get bigger and heavier until, in the end, they are too heavy to float, and fall to the ground as rain.

- Have you ever heard of showers of frogs or fish? Well, they do happen. The animals are sometimes sucked up from ponds by extra-strong winds. Later on, they fall to the ground with the rain.

How cold is snow?

Snowflakes are water droplets that have frozen into crystals of ice. To stay frozen, they have to be at freezing point – that's 0 °C. If they get any warmer than this, snowflakes melt and fall to the ground as rain.

- The biggest snowman ever built was more than 22 metres high. That's about as tall as a seven-storey building.

Where do thunderstorms start?

Thunderstorms start in the huge black thunderclouds that sometimes gather at the end of a hot summer's day. Inside the clouds, strong winds hurl the water droplets around, and the cloud crackles with electricity. It flashes through the sky in great dazzling sparks, which we call lightning.

- It's safest to stay inside during a thunderstorm. Never shelter under a tree – it might get struck by lightning.

- An American man was struck by lightning seven times! Roy C. Sullivan had his hair set alight twice and his eyebrows burnt off. He even lost a big toenail.

- Lightning can travel as far as 140,000 kilometres in 1 second flat!

- To find out how far away a storm is, count the number of seconds between the lightning and the thunder. The storm is 1 kilometre away for every 3 seconds you count.

- The biggest thunderclouds tower 16 kilometres into the air. That's nearly twice the height of Mount Everest.

What is thunder?

Sparks of lightning are incredibly hot. As they flash through the sky, they heat the air so quickly that it makes a loud booming noise like an explosion. This is thunder.

What is a tornado?

A tornado is a spinning twist of wind which speeds across the ground, sucking up everything in its path. Tornadoes happen mainly in North America.

Hurricanes are another kind of spinning storm, but they begin over warm tropical seas. Hurricane winds can blow at speeds of up to 240 kilometres per hour.

● In the USA, in 1931, a tornado lifted a train into the air and dumped it in a ditch.

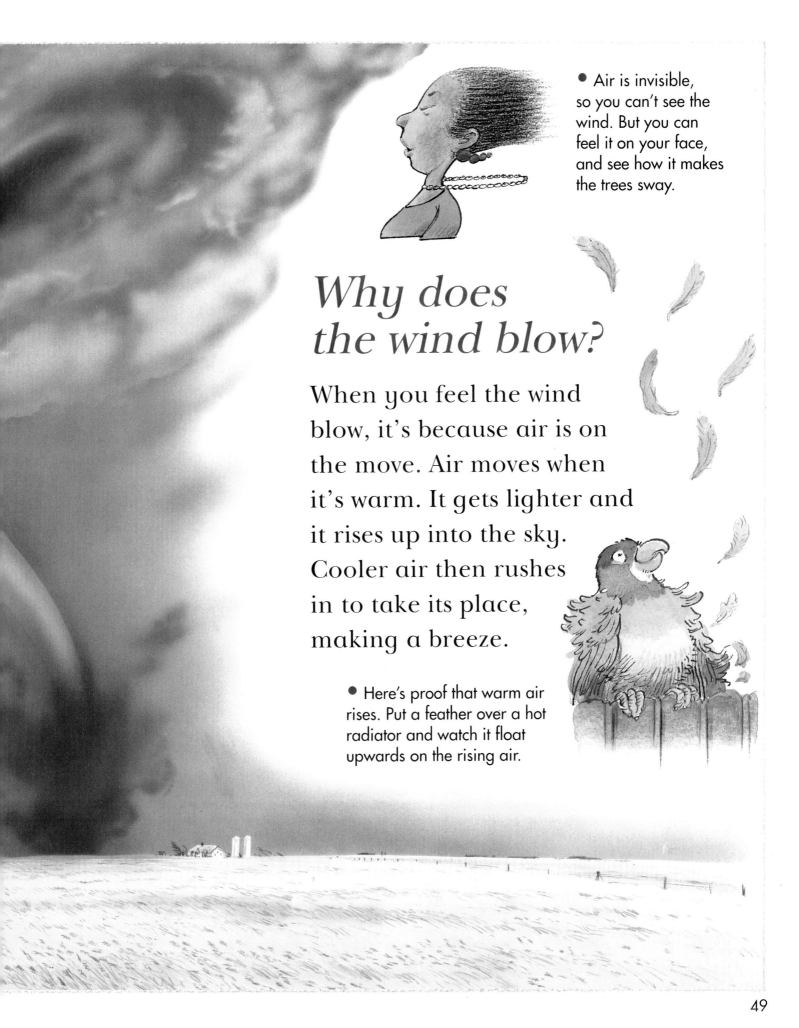

- Air is invisible, so you can't see the wind. But you can feel it on your face, and see how it makes the trees sway.

Why does the wind blow?

When you feel the wind blow, it's because air is on the move. Air moves when it's warm. It gets lighter and it rises up into the sky. Cooler air then rushes in to take its place, making a breeze.

- Here's proof that warm air rises. Put a feather over a hot radiator and watch it float upwards on the rising air.

How big is the ocean?

The ocean is truly ENORMOUS! It covers more than twice as much of the Earth as land does. In fact, it's made up of four oceans – the Pacific, the Atlantic, the Indian and the Arctic. Although these all have different names, they flow into each other to make one huge world ocean.

● Don't go for a swim in the Arctic Ocean. It's the coldest of the oceans, and for most of the year it's covered in ice.

Which is the biggest ocean?

The Pacific is by far the biggest ocean in the world. It's larger than the other three oceans put together, and it's also much deeper. If you look at a globe, you'll see that the Pacific reaches halfway around the world.

What's the difference between a sea and an ocean?

People often use the words sea and ocean to mean the same thing. That's fine, but to a scientist, seas are just part of an ocean – the parts that are nearest to land. The Mediterranean Sea is between Africa and Europe, for example.

● These drops of water show the oceans in order of size.

Pacific

Atlantic

Indian

Arctic

What makes waves roll?

● Make your own waves in a bowl of water. The harder you blow across the surface, the bigger the waves.

Waves are ripples of water blown across the surface of the ocean by the wind. On a calm day they hardly move, but in stormy weather they roll faster and faster, and grow higher and higher, until they form huge walls of water.

● Some waves are called white horses because their curly white tips look like horses' manes.

● At Waimea Bay, Hawaii, surfers ride waves up to 10 metres high – that's six times taller than a man!

SCIENCE
AND THE
HUMAN BODY

What is science about?

Science is all about discovering how and why things happen in the world around you. It's about everyday things like finding out where water goes when it boils, as well as more complicated things like why we need water to live.

3 Put some water in the freezer and leave it for an hour or two. What do you notice when you take it out? The water isn't liquid any more – it's a solid, and you can't pour solids.

2 Now fill a jug with water and pour it into a cup. Most liquids will pour, but some move faster than others. Try pouring some honey into a saucer – does it move as quickly as water?

1 The kitchen is a great place for scientists. Start by turning on a tap and looking at the water that flows out. Runny things like water are called liquids.

What do scientists do?

One of the first things scientists do is to ask questions. Then they try to answer the questions by looking closely at things and testing out their ideas. We call this experimenting. Scientists sometimes manage to come up with the answers – but not always!

4 All liquids can change shape, but most solids can't. Pour some water into a jelly mould and it will fill up all the nooks and crannies. What happens when you put ice cubes in?

5 Ask a grown-up to put a cup of water into a saucepan and boil it for you for 5 minutes. Lots of steam comes off, doesn't it? Let the water cool, then pour it back into the cup. There's less water now – where has the rest gone?

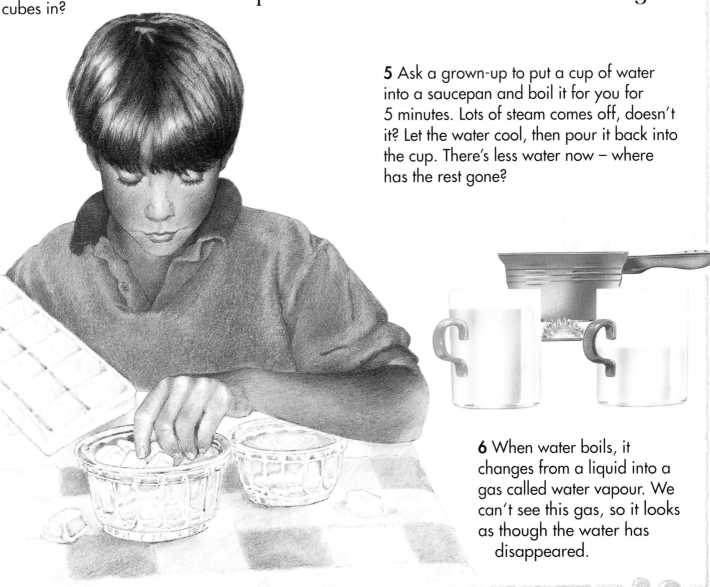

6 When water boils, it changes from a liquid into a gas called water vapour. We can't see this gas, so it looks as though the water has disappeared.

Why do I run out of energy?

• When you run, the stored energy in your body is changed into movement energy.

You run out of energy because you use it! Walking, running and jumping all need energy – without it you wouldn't be able to talk, write, read or even sleep! Energy is stored inside your body and comes from your food. That's why you get hungry – your body is telling you to put back some of the energy you've used.

• Lots of things give out energy, in many different forms. Here are just some of them.

Fire = heat energy

Bike = movement energy

Drum = sound energy

● Eating a small apple gives you enough energy to sleep for half an hour.

● Energy is never made or destroyed. It just changes from one form to another. Bending a bow stores energy in the bow. This changes into movement energy as the arrow flies from the bow.

What is energy?

Energy makes things happen – nothing in the universe would work without it. You can't see energy, but you can see what it does to things around you. Because of energy, cars move and planes fly, lamps give out light, drums make music, and fires give off heat.

Food = chemical energy

Train = electrical energy

Torch = light energy

Why does the spoon get hot when I stir my cocoa?

Heat energy never stays still. It is always moving. The teaspoon warms up when you stir your cocoa because heat energy is moving from the hot drink into the spoon.

● Things that allow heat to pass through them easily are called conductors. A metal spoon is a good conductor.

● Our bodies give off heat all the time. Some burglar alarms work by picking up the heat given off by a burglar's body.

Why is sunlight warm?

Sunlight is warm because the Sun gives off heat as well as light energy. The Sun's heat energy travels towards us in invisible straight lines called heat rays. You can't see them, of course, but you can feel them on your skin on hot sunny days.

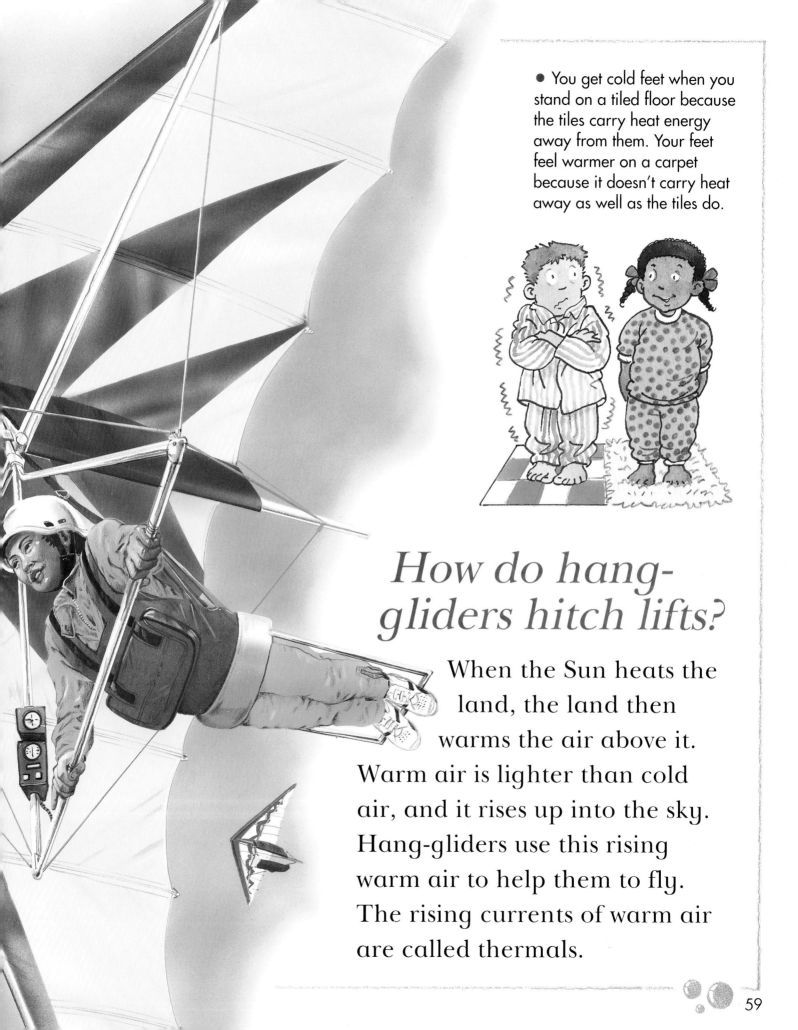

● You get cold feet when you stand on a tiled floor because the tiles carry heat energy away from them. Your feet feel warmer on a carpet because it doesn't carry heat away as well as the tiles do.

How do hang-gliders hitch lifts?

When the Sun heats the land, the land then warms the air above it. Warm air is lighter than cold air, and it rises up into the sky. Hang-gliders use this rising warm air to help them to fly. The rising currents of warm air are called thermals.

What is sound?

Sound is a type of energy. It happens when something shakes or moves back and forwards really quickly. The shaking movements are called vibrations. You hear sounds because vibrations travel through the air into your ears.

- Some singers can sing a note which is so high and so loud that it breaks a glass!

- Here's a way to see how sounds vibrate. Tie a piece of thread to some tissue paper. Now, put on some loud music and hold the thread in front of a loud-speaker. The vibrations should make the tissue paper shake. If they don't, turn up the music!

- Crashing a pair of cymbals together makes them vibrate, sending out ringing sounds.

Why do trumpeters blow raspberries?

Blowing raspberries is the only way to get sounds out of a trumpet! It makes a trumpeter's lips vibrate, and this makes the air inside the trumpet shake, too. The air comes out the other end as a musical note!

● Sound travels through air at 340 metres per second. That's nearly the length of four football pitches.

Can sound travel under water?

● Sound needs something to travel through – air, water, or some other material. There's no air in space, so astronauts have to use radios to talk to one another.

Yes, it can! Sound moves four times faster through water than through air. It can travel such long distances that whales can hear each other when they are over a hundred kilometres apart.

What is air made of?

● You're using air when you take a deep breath and blow out the candles on a cake!

Air is a mixture of gases – mostly nitrogen and oxygen, with a little bit of carbon dioxide and some water vapour. It also has tiny bits of salt, dust and dirt. You can't see, smell or taste the air, but you can feel it when the wind blows.

● We don't notice it, but the air around us is heavy, and pushes down on us. The air in a medium-sized room weighs as much as 70 cans of baked beans!

How do bubbles get into fizzy drinks?

The bubbles in fizzy drinks are made of carbon dioxide. The gas is squashed into the bottle so hard that it disappears into the drink. When the bottle is opened, the bubbles have room to escape and start fizzing into the air.

● Make your own bubbles of carbon dioxide gas by adding a teaspoon of baking powder to a beaker of water. Stand by for the fizz!

Why do cakes rise?

When you put a cake in the oven, the mixture heats up and makes bubbles of carbon dioxide. These grow bigger in the heat, and make the cake rise.

● The air you beat into a cake mixture also helps to make the cake deliciously light.

Why do shadows happen?

Light travels in straight lines called rays. When the rays hit something that they can't shine through, the light is blocked, and a dark shadow forms on the other side.

• Try to make animal shadows on a wall by wiggling your fingers in the beam of a bright torch.

• There are lots of things that light can't shine through – walls, furniture, your own body, for example. We call these things opaque.

• Light is another kind of energy. Plants use the energy in sunlight to make food for themselves in their leaves. Sunflowers get all the sunlight they can by turning to face the Sun as it moves across the sky.

• Did you know that you can use shadows to tell the time? Next time it's sunny, stand a pencil inside a cotton reel on a piece of paper. Every hour, draw a line along the pencil's shadow, and write down the time. Now you can use your shadow clock to tell the time on every sunny day.

Why can I see through glass?

You can see through glass because it's transparent – that means it's clear, and it lets the light shine through. Glass is great for windows because it lets sunlight into a room, and allows you to see what's going on in the world outside!

• Bathroom windows are often made of frosted glass. This still lets some light through, but the frosting stops people from seeing straight through the glass.

Can light bounce?

When rays of light hit something that they can't shine through, they bounce off it – just like a ball bouncing off the ground. This is called reflection. We are able to see things because light is reflected off them into our eyes.

● You can see yourself when you look down into a puddle because the smooth water reflects the light straight back into your eyes.

● Up periscope! A submarine officer looks through a periscope to see what's happening above the water. Mirrors inside the periscope reflect light from things above the water straight down into the officer's eyes.

● The Moon reflects light from the Sun. It has no light of its own.

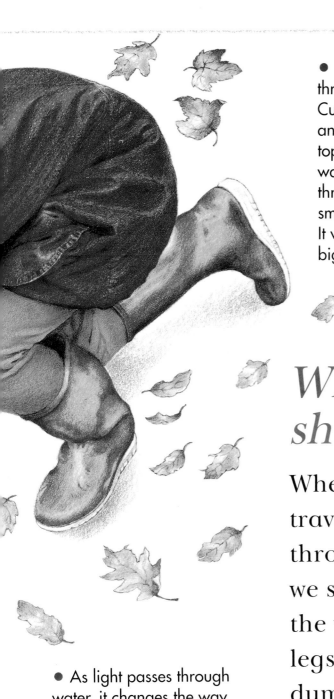

● See what happens when light passes through a single drop of water. Cut a hole in a piece of card and stick clear tape over the top. Carefully put a drop of water on the tape and look through it at something small, like a ladybird. It will make it look bigger.

Why do my legs look shorter under water?

When light enters water, its rays travel more slowly than they do through the air. This changes the way we see things. Looking down through the water in a swimming pool, your legs look very short and dumpy. Don't worry – they aren't really!

● As light passes through water, it changes the way we see things. This makes it tricky to net fish – they aren't where they appear to be. To catch one, you have to aim below the place where you actually see it.

Why do rainbows happen?

Although sunlight looks white, it's really made up of lots of different colours. During a shower of rain, the Sun sometimes shines through the tiny raindrops that fall through the air. When this happens, the water makes the light spread into all its different colours. The colours always appear in the same order, and a beautiful rainbow forms in the sky.

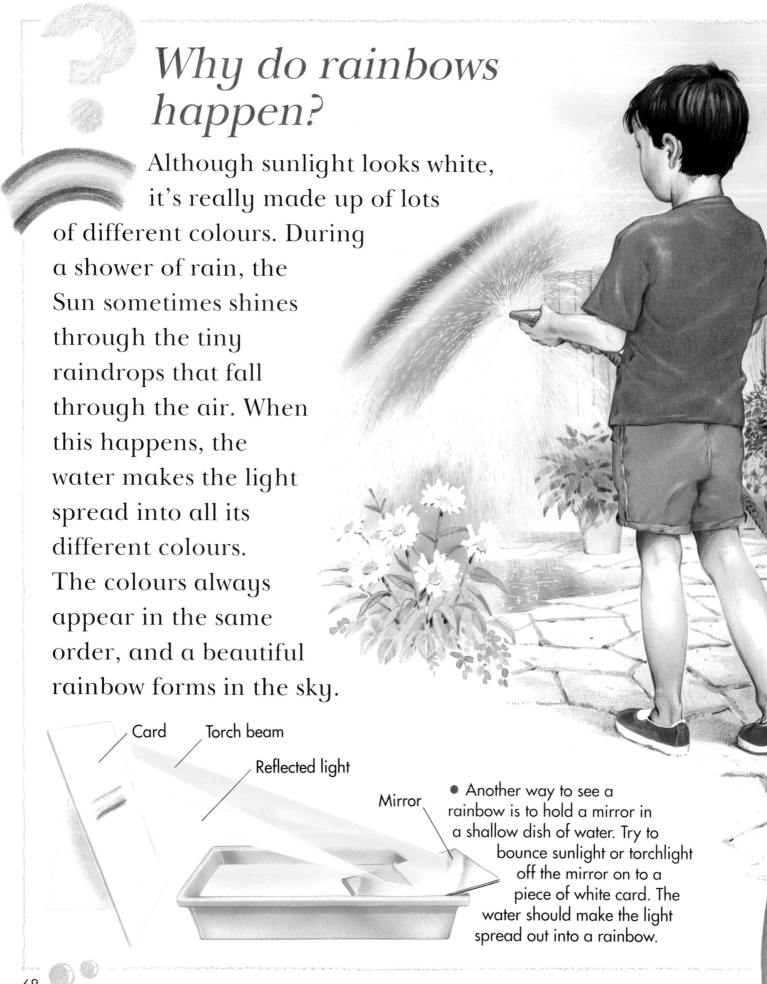

Card

Torch beam

Reflected light

Mirror

● Another way to see a rainbow is to hold a mirror in a shallow dish of water. Try to bounce sunlight or torchlight off the mirror on to a piece of white card. The water should make the light spread out into a rainbow.

- You don't have to wait for rain to see a rainbow. Water the garden on a sunny day, and you may see rainbow colours in the spray.

Why is grass green?

We see things when light reflects off them into our eyes. But not all of white light's colours are reflected. Some are soaked up. Grass looks green because it soaks up all the colours in white light apart from green.

- The bright colours of many animals often work as a warning. The black and yellow stripes on a wasp warn us – and other animals – to keep away from its poisonous sting.

Can cats see in colour?

- Many animals don't really need to see in colour. They rely far more on their sharp hearing and sense of smell.

Yes, they can – but they don't see all the colours that you do! Cats don't really need to see bright colours, as most of them are busiest at night, outdoors hunting for food.

What can walk on water?

Tiny insects called pond-skaters are so light that they can walk across water without sinking into it! But even pond-skaters wouldn't get anywhere without a force called surface tension. This pulls on the surface of the water, making a thin stretchy 'skin' on the top.

● Raindrops aren't quite round – they're almost flat underneath.

Why are water droplets round?

Small drops of water are almost perfectly round because they are pulled into this shape by surface tension. Bigger drops spread out, though – they're too heavy for surface tension to work so well.

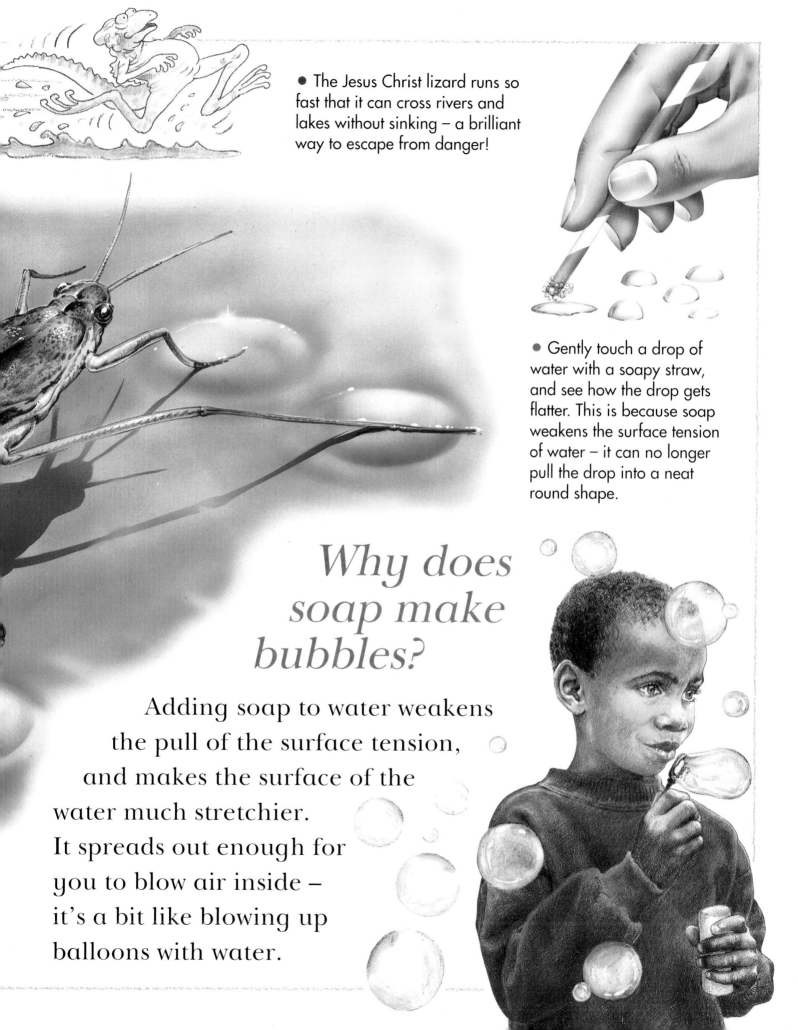

● The Jesus Christ lizard runs so fast that it can cross rivers and lakes without sinking – a brilliant way to escape from danger!

● Gently touch a drop of water with a soapy straw, and see how the drop gets flatter. This is because soap weakens the surface tension of water – it can no longer pull the drop into a neat round shape.

Why does soap make bubbles?

Adding soap to water weakens the pull of the surface tension, and makes the surface of the water much stretchier. It spreads out enough for you to blow air inside – it's a bit like blowing up balloons with water.

Why do we need air?

All the animals on Earth need to breathe the oxygen in air to stay alive – and that includes you! That's because bodies use oxygen to make energy for living and growing.

● All plants need air, light and water to live and grow. So do people, and every other living thing on our planet.

● Even though they live in the sea, whales breathe oxygen from the air. Sperm whales can hold their breath for up to two hours before coming up for air.

Why do we need light?

Without the Sun's light, there would be nothing to eat! Plants are the only living things that can make their own food, and they need sunlight to do this. Everything else on Earth feeds on plants, or on plant-eating animals. If there weren't any plants, we'd all starve to death!

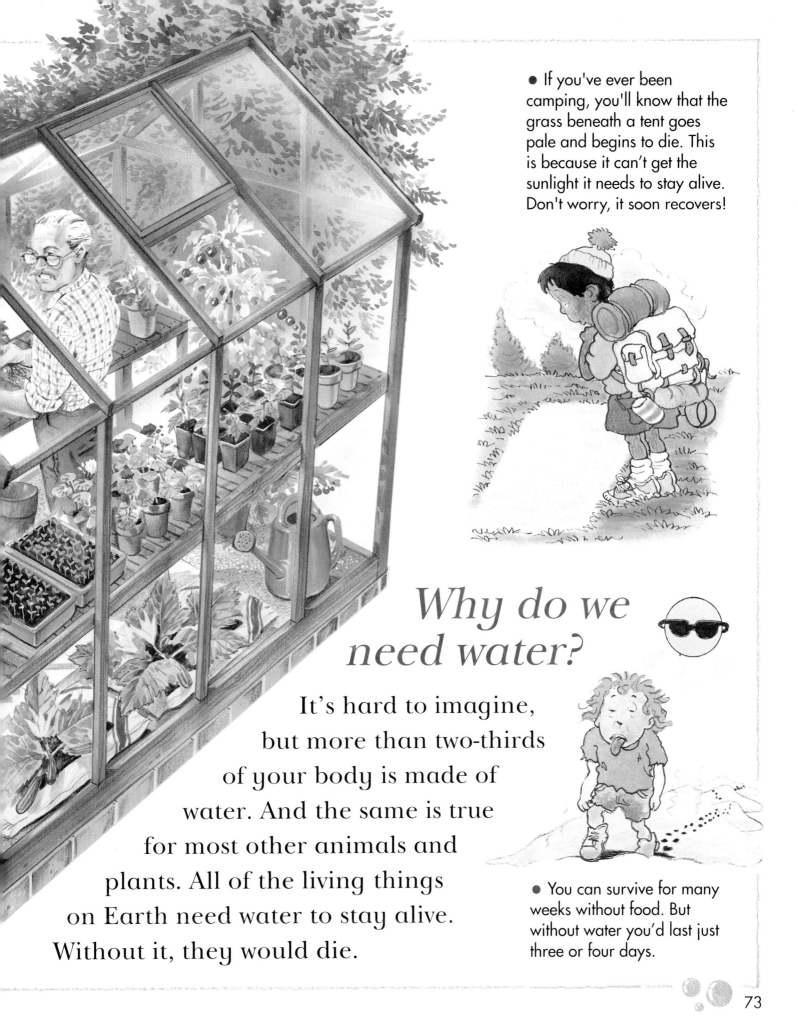

• If you've ever been camping, you'll know that the grass beneath a tent goes pale and begins to die. This is because it can't get the sunlight it needs to stay alive. Don't worry, it soon recovers!

Why do we need water?

It's hard to imagine, but more than two-thirds of your body is made of water. And the same is true for most other animals and plants. All of the living things on Earth need water to stay alive. Without it, they would die.

• You can survive for many weeks without food. But without water you'd last just three or four days.

Where do I come from?

You began when a tiny egg inside your mother (no bigger than a full stop) joined with a tiny bit of your father, called a sperm. Then you grew and grew until you were big enough to be born.

- You stayed in your mother's womb for about nine months. As you got bigger, her womb stretched to make space for you.

Womb

Sperm

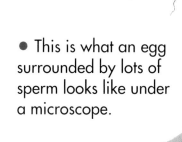

- This is what an egg surrounded by lots of sperm looks like under a microscope.

Egg

Womb

- In the womb, you floated in a kind of bag filled with water which kept you safe and warm.

- You grew inside your mother in a part of her body called the womb.

- When you were ready to be born, the opening of your mother's womb stretched to let you out.

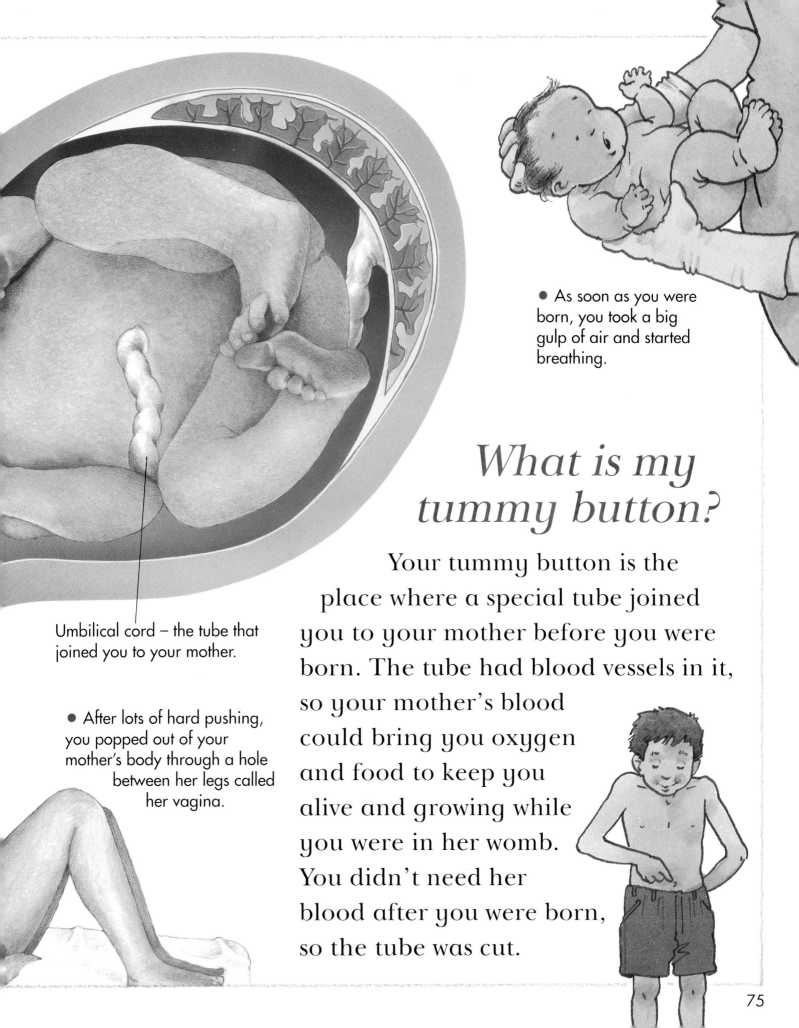

Umbilical cord – the tube that joined you to your mother.

● As soon as you were born, you took a big gulp of air and started breathing.

● After lots of hard pushing, you popped out of your mother's body through a hole between her legs called her vagina.

What is my tummy button?

Your tummy button is the place where a special tube joined you to your mother before you were born. The tube had blood vessels in it, so your mother's blood could bring you oxygen and food to keep you alive and growing while you were in her womb. You didn't need her blood after you were born, so the tube was cut.

How many bones do I have?

When you were born, you had about 350 bones. But by the time you finish growing, you will have just over 200!

The missing bones won't have fallen out or disappeared. Instead, as you get older, some of your smaller bones will join together to make bigger ones.

● Without bones inside you to give you a shape, you'd be like a floppy, squishy bag.

Thigh bone

● The longest bone in your body is the one above your knee, called your thigh bone.

● Your bones are partly made of a hard stony stuff called calcium, but unlike stones they are alive. They get bigger as you grow up.

Foot bones

• Most of us have twelve pairs of ribs, but some people have an extra one. Your ribs help to keep your lungs and heart safe.

• Although your skull is made of lots of bones, most of them are fixed together. Only your jaw bone moves.

• Bones are hard and strong. They help to keep the softer parts inside you (like your brain) from getting hurt.

Breast bone

Ribs

Backbone

Hip bones

Skull

Arm bones

Hand bones

What is my funny bone?

The funny thing about your funny bone is that it isn't a bone at all. It's a nerve that runs just under your skin over each elbow. If you bang your elbow, the nerve is banged, too. It sends a message to your brain and you feel pain!

How do I move?

Muscles make you move, by pulling your bones about. When you smile or cry, speak or eat, walk or skip, muscles are doing the work.

● A muscle can only make itself shorter. It needs another muscle pulling the other way to stretch it out again.

● Your biggest muscles are the ones you sit on!

Why do strong people have big muscles?

● Many tennis players have bigger muscles in the arm they use to hold their racket.

Muscles get bigger and stronger if they are used a lot. That's why sportswomen and men practise hard and do lots of exercises.

• To make a bone move, a muscle gets shorter. This pulls the bone one way. To pull the bone back again, another muscle gets shorter. Muscles are fixed to your bones by strong white strings called tendons.

This muscle tightens to bend your arm.

Tendon

When this muscle tightens, your arm straightens.

What is cramp?

Cramp is when a muscle suddenly feels tight and painful. It stops moving properly and it feels like it's stuck. No one is quite sure why cramp happens, but it goes away if you rest the sore part. Rubbing it can also help.

• Have you ever had a stitch after running? It's a pain in your middle, just under your ribs. It means you've got cramp in the breathing muscle below your lungs.

79

What does my heart do?

Your heart is a very special muscle which keeps blood moving around your body.

If you put your hand on your chest near your heart, you'll feel it beating. Each time it beats, it pumps blood out around your body.

● To hear a heart beating, find somewhere quiet and rest your ear against a friend's chest. You should hear two sounds close together – 'lub-dub', 'lub-dub', 'lub-dub'.

● Blood travels round your body in thin tubes called blood vessels.

● Your body is using up oxygen all the time, keeping you alive, so it has to keep getting more from your lungs.

Blood from your head

To the body

Blood from your body

- One side of your heart pumps blood to your lungs to get oxygen. The other side pumps it around your body.

Blood to your lungs

Blood from your lungs

Blood with oxygen

Blood without oxygen

What is blood for?

Your blood is like a fast-moving river flowing around your body. It carries useful things – like oxygen from the air you breathe, and the goodness from the food you eat – to every part of you. It also helps your body to fight germs.

- When you were a baby, you had less than a litre of blood – not quite enough to fill a milk carton. When you grow up, you will have about five litres of blood – enough to half fill a bucket!

How big is my heart?

Our hearts grow with us – they get bigger as we do. Whatever size you are now, your heart will be a bit bigger than your fist.

- Some insects have blue or green blood.

What is inside my head?

The most exciting and important part of your body is hidden inside your head, beneath your hair, your skin and your hard skull bone. It is your brain.

Your brain is the part of you that thinks and remembers. It also makes sure the rest of your body is doing what it should!

● Your brain has two sides. The right side of your brain looks after the left side of your body, while the left side looks after the right side of your body.

● People's brains come in different sizes. But bigger brains don't make people more clever – any more than having big feet makes them better runners!

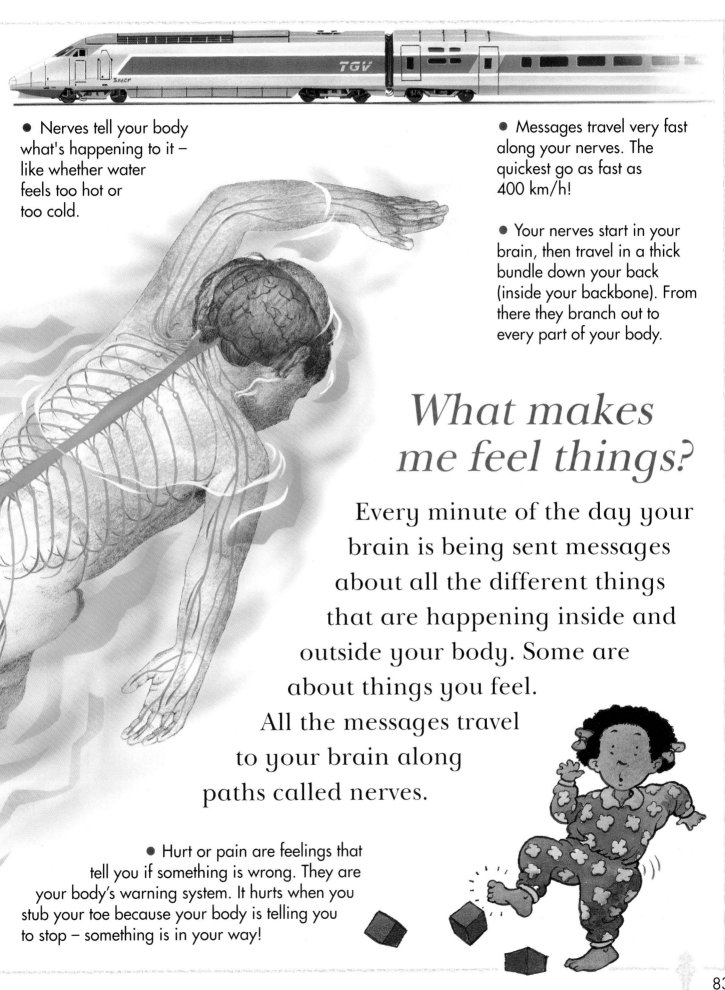

- Nerves tell your body what's happening to it – like whether water feels too hot or too cold.

- Messages travel very fast along your nerves. The quickest go as fast as 400 km/h!

- Your nerves start in your brain, then travel in a thick bundle down your back (inside your backbone). From there they branch out to every part of your body.

What makes me feel things?

Every minute of the day your brain is being sent messages about all the different things that are happening inside and outside your body. Some are about things you feel. All the messages travel to your brain along paths called nerves.

- Hurt or pain are feelings that tell you if something is wrong. They are your body's warning system. It hurts when you stub your toe because your body is telling you to stop – something is in your way!

Why do I breathe?

You pull air into your body when you breathe. And air is something your body cannot do without, even for just a few minutes.

This is because air has a gas called oxygen in it, and your body needs oxygen to live and grow.

● When you breathe in, air goes down your windpipe to your lungs. These are like big sponges which hold air instead of water.

● If you fold your arms across your chest and breathe in, you'll feel your lungs getting bigger as they fill up with air.

Windpipe

Lungs

84

What makes me hiccup?

There's a big muscle below your lungs which helps you to breathe. It's called your diaphragm muscle. You hiccup when something makes this muscle pull down really hard, drawing lots of air into your lungs. To stop too much air rushing in, a flap at the top of your windpipe clamps down. This closes off the air flow so quickly that your whole body jerks.

● 'HIC' is air rushing in.

● 'CUP' is the flap clamping down over your windpipe.

What makes me sneeze?

If dust or germs get into your nose, your body makes you sneeze to get rid of them. Your lungs shoot air out, clearing your nose.

● When you sneeze, air rushes down your nose at over 160 kilometres per hour!

Why do I blink?

Your eyes make tears all the time, not only when you cry. Blinking spreads the tears across your eyes and stops them from drying out and getting sore.

● The iris is the coloured part of your eye. It works rather like curtains on a window – when it's too dark to see, the iris opens to let in more light. When the light is too bright, the iris tightens up to protect the eye.

● A blink lasts for about one-third of a second. You do it thousands of times a day.

● Eyelashes help to stop things like dust and grit getting into your eyes.

Eyelash

Pupil

Iris

● The black hole in the middle of the eye is called the pupil.

• Jelly-like stuff in your eyeball keeps it in shape, like air in a balloon.

Why can't I see in the dark?

You can't see much when it's dark, because eyes need light to see. If you look at your eyes in a mirror, you'll see a black hole in the middle of them. Light bounces off everything around you and in through this hole. Messages are then sent from your eyes to your brain, telling you what you are looking at.

• The lining at the back of the eye is called the retina. The picture that forms here is upside down! Your brain turns it the right way up.

A nerve inside here carries messages to your brain.

• There's a lens at the front of the eye. It makes sure the things you see aren't fuzzy, by making light shine in the right place at the back of the eye.

Why are ears such a funny shape?

The shape of your ears helps them to catch sounds from the air. The sounds then go through your ear hole into the hidden part of your ear, inside your head. Animals like rabbits can move their ears to help them catch sounds.

Why do I feel dizzy when I spin round?

Inside each ear, you have three loop-shaped tubes with watery liquid in them. This swishes about when you spin round. Special nerves pick up this movement and tell your brain you are spinning. If you stop suddenly, the liquid still swishes about for a bit. Your brain gets the wrong message and you feel dizzy!

Ear lobe

● Did you know that you have a drum in your ear? Your ear drum is a bit of thin skin which moves very quickly when sounds hit it.

● When your ear drum moves, it makes three tiny bones wobble.

● When the bones wobble, they make watery liquid deep inside your ear move about, too. Special nerves pick up this movement and send messages to your brain.

This nerve carries messages from ear to brain.

These tubes help you to balance.

Stirrup bone

Anvil bone

Hammer bone

Ear canal

Ear drum

● The smallest bone in your body is in your ear. It is called the stirrup, and it is about 2 millimetres from one end to the other – small enough to sit on top of this letter u.

● If you hold a shell to your ear, you'll hear the sound of the blood flowing around inside your head. It sounds a bit like the sea.

What is my nose for?

Your nose is for smelling things, and it also helps your tongue with tasting. It can do this because tiny bits of food are carried by air up into your nose when you eat.

The bits are far too small to see, but nerves inside your nose find them and send messages about them to your brain.

● When a cold bungs your nose up, air can't get to the nose nerves and you can't taste your food properly.

● Here's a way to see how much you taste things with your nose. You'll need someone to help you.

1 Get two different flavours of fruit yogurt.

2 Shut your eyes tight and hold your nose.

3 See if you can tell which yogurt you are eating.

● To see how your tongue helps you to speak, put your finger on it and try to say 'Hello'.

What is my tongue for?

Your tongue is for tasting things, but it also helps you to speak and sing. It is covered with tiny little bumps called tastebuds, which send messages along nerves to your brain about all the delicious things you eat or drink.

Why do teeth fall out?

● When you are grown up, you will have between 28 and 32 teeth.

As you grow up, most parts of your body get bigger. But your teeth can't grow bigger, and so you have to change them.

When you are small, you have twenty small teeth called milk teeth. These start to fall out when you are five or six years old, to let new, bigger teeth grow in their place.

Why do I get ill sometimes?

When a part of your body stops working properly, you get ill. You don't feel right. Perhaps your tummy hurts, or you may have lots of itchy spots on your skin. Illness often happens because things called germs get inside your body.

● Sometimes your body has to fight and kill germs. The doctor may give you medicine to help it to do this.

● Some germs like dirt. Washing your body and cleaning your teeth help to keep these germs away.

TRANSPORT AND BUILDINGS

How far can I go in an hour?

If you keep walking for an hour, and don't stop to take any rests, your own two legs will carry you about 4 kilometres. You'll be able to go farther if you run, but you'll probably have to keep stopping to get your breath back. The easiest way to travel more than a few kilometres in an hour is to get something to carry you!

● It would take an ordinary garden snail more than three days to get as far as you can walk in one hour.

● Trotting on a pony for an hour, you'd be able to travel three times as far as you would on foot.

● To walk as far as a jumbo jet can carry you in an hour, you'd have to keep going for more than ten whole days and nights!

● Racing cyclists can pedal at least ten times as fast as you can walk. They can cover as much as 40 kilometres in an hour.

● Aircraft are the fastest way to travel. Flying high above the clouds in a jumbo jet, you'd be able to get from Paris to London in less than an hour.

● Riding in a high-speed train like the Japanese Bullet train or the French TGV, you can travel at least twice as fast as you could in a car.

● Engines are more powerful than muscles, so machines can carry you much faster than legs. Riding in a car on a motorway, you can travel at more than 100 kilometres an hour!

● Even if you stay in bed all day, you will travel about 2.5 million kilometres! That's how far the Earth moves through space in 24 hours, as it goes around the Sun.

Which is the fastest car?

A British car called *Thrust 2* set the world land speed record in 1983. Using an aircraft jet engine in place of a normal car engine, it reached nearly 1020 kilometres an hour.

- The first car to go faster than 100 kilometres an hour was battery-powered. It was called *La Jamais Contente*, and it did this nearly 100 years ago, in 1899.

- The world's fastest sailing craft are sailboards. In good winds, they can zip across the water at more than 80 kilometres an hour.

Spirit of Australia

Which is the fastest boat?

Hydroplanes skim over the water almost as if flying. In 1977, Ken Warby roared to 556 kilometres an hour in his jet-powered *Spirit of Australia.*

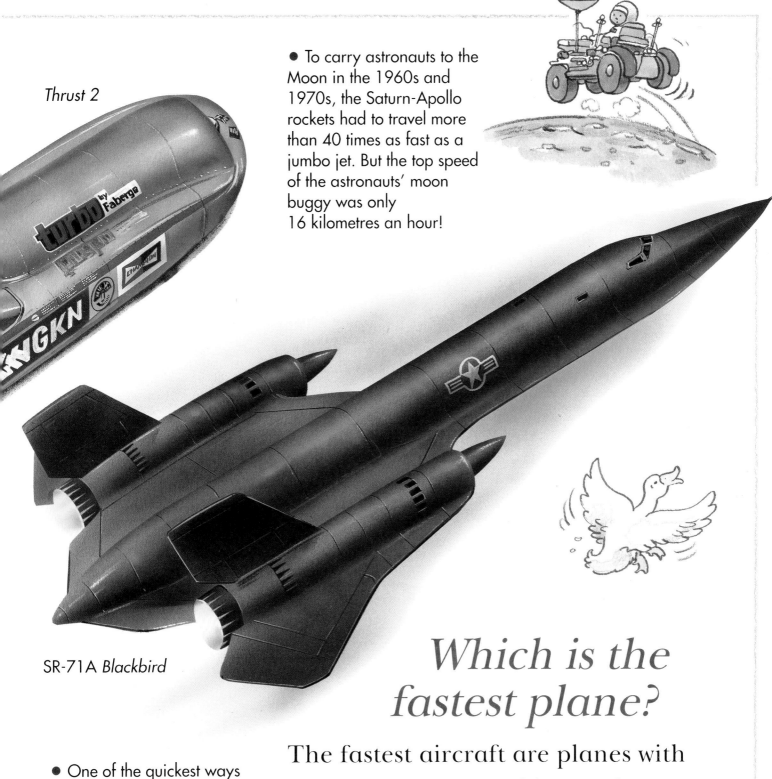

Thrust 2

• To carry astronauts to the Moon in the 1960s and 1970s, the Saturn-Apollo rockets had to travel more than 40 times as fast as a jumbo jet. But the top speed of the astronauts' moon buggy was only 16 kilometres an hour!

SR-71A _Blackbird_

Which is the fastest plane?

• One of the quickest ways to travel without an engine is on skis.

The fastest aircraft are planes with jet engines. The world record was set back in 1976, when the USA's SR-71A reached an amazing 3530 kilometres an hour! It was nicknamed _Blackbird_.

Which plane can waggle its nose?

The superfast passenger jet Concorde can move its nose. With its long slim nose sticking straight out, Concorde can slip through the air at well over double the speed of a jumbo jet. However, when Concorde lands, its nose has to be lowered out of the way. If this isn't done, the pilot can't see the runway!

● Concorde heats up so much in flight that its body stretches – it can get as much as 28 centimetres longer.

● The world's largest passenger planes, the Boeing 747s, are nicknamed jumbo jets after an elephant. Jumbo was a star attraction at London Zoo in the 1800s.

Can planes move their wings?

Yes, some fighter planes have wings that can be moved in and out. This is because wings that stick straight out are the best shape for taking off and landing, and for flying slowly. When wings swing back, they give the plane a smoother shape, which helps it to cut through the air at top speed.

● Birds have the best swing wings of all. A peregrine falcon holds its wings out to hover over its prey, then tucks them back to dive down for the kill. It can reach 300 kilometres an hour in its dive.

● Harrier fighter planes have been nicknamed jump jets because they can take off straight up into the air.

Do airships run on air?

Modern airships should really be called gas ships, because they use a gas called helium to help them to fly. Helium helps airships to float because it is lighter than air.

The bag of an airship is called an envelope.

● Fairground balloons are usually filled with helium gas. To see which is lighter, helium or air, try letting go of a fairground balloon at the same time as a party balloon filled with air.

● The first `air' letter was carried by a balloon.

● The first-ever balloon passengers were a cock, a duck and a sheep! Their 8-minute flight took place over Paris in 1783, more than 200 years ago.

Burner

Why do hot-air balloons float?

Balloons float because hot air rises, and hot air rises because it is lighter than cold air. The air inside a hot-air balloon is heated by a burner, which works rather like a camping gas stove.

Why do cars have wheels?

Cars and most other land machines have wheels because they make it easier to move. Things slow down when they rub against the ground. Wheels help because they turn easily, and only a small part of them touches the ground.

- Imagine how difficult it would be to move a car if all of it was touching the ground, instead of just its wheels!

- The world's longest car has 26 wheels! It even has room for a tiny swimming pool on board!

- Snow and ice are much more slippery than soil and rock. That's why skis and ice-skates don't need wheels!

Which are the biggest tyres?

The world's biggest tyres are made for huge dumper trucks, to cushion their heavy loads of rock and earth. The tyres are over 3.6 metres high – that's about three times as tall as you are!

● The wheelbarrow was invented in China more than 1800 years ago. It made it easier to carry heavy loads.

Which ships have wheels?

River boats called paddle-steamers are driven along by wheels. The wheels have wide boards called paddles. As the wheels turn, the paddles push against the water, moving the boat along.

Why do cars need petrol?

A car needs petrol for the same reason that you need food – to give it energy to move. It's hard to tell by looking at it, but petrol has lots of energy locked up inside it. This energy is set free inside a car engine, so it can be used to turn road wheels.

● Many toy cars use electrical energy, stored in batteries. There are a few ordinary cars that run on batteries, too.

● Petrol is made from oil, and it has energy because it comes from things that were once living! Oil formed millions of years ago, from the bodies of tiny plants and animals.

Exhaust pipe

Petrol tank

● Petrol is kept in a tank. It is pumped along a pipe to the engine.

Pistons

What happens inside car engines?

Petrol is mixed with air inside a car engine and then set on fire by an electric spark. This makes the air and petrol explode with a bang.

This explosion pushes engine parts called pistons up and down very quickly. The pistons make a rod called the crankshaft spin round. The crankshaft makes other rods spin, and they turn the road wheels.

Spark plug

Spark

Piston

Cylinder

Crankshaft

● Each piston moves up and down inside a cylinder.

Do road trains run on rails?

No, road trains run on roads. They are called trains because they are made up of trucks pulling lots of trailers, in the same way that locomotives haul wagons.

● Not all trains need drivers. Some city trains are controlled by computers.

● Australian trucks and cars often have strong metal bull-bars fitted in front, to cut down damage if they hit large animals such as kangaroos or cattle on outback roads. Another name for them is roo bars ('roo' is short for kangaroo).

● Trams are buses with metal wheels that run on rails. They use electricity to move, taking it from cables stretched high above the road.

Bull-bars

● Road trains are often used in areas where there are no railway lines – in parts of the Australian Outback, for example.

Can trains fly?

Maglevs are a new kind of passenger train which float just above a special track. They are lifted and driven by the power of magnets, and they can travel very fast – at over 400 kilometres an hour!

Why don't ships sink?

When things are put into water they make room for themselves by pushing it aside. Although ships are heavy, they are hollow with high sides. This means they can settle quite low in the water, pushing a lot of it aside. In fact, a ship won't sink unless it is overloaded and becomes heavier than the water it pushes aside.

● You push water aside when you get into a bath. That's why you have to be careful not to overfill it!

How do submarines sink?

GOING UP

Air in

GOING DOWN

Air out

Water out

Water in

Submarines sink by making themselves too heavy to float. Water is let into special tanks to add weight. When it's time for the submarine to resurface, the water is pumped out.

Which ships fly?

Although hovercraft travel across water, they don't float in it like ships. Instead, they hover just above the waves, held up by a cushion of air.

● Hovercraft can travel over land as well as water.

● This strange-looking diving suit was invented over 200 years ago. The tubes carried air to and from the surface.

● One of the earliest submarines was built by Dutchman Cornelius van Drebbel and tested in the 1620s. Twelve oarsmen rowed a wooden boat below the surface of the Thames River, in England.

Which plane rides piggyback?

It's not every day that you see a plane riding piggyback, but it does happen. The Shuttle orbiter carries people into space and back again. When it returns to Earth from space it sometimes lands in California in the USA, thousands of kilometres from its take-off base in Florida. To get back home again, it rides piggyback on a jumbo jet.

● Ships can ride piggyback, too, on special heavy-lift ships! First, the heavy-lift ship makes itself sink – not completely, but low enough for a smaller ship to float on to its deck. When it rises up again, the smaller ship gets a ride.

1

2

3

When do cars hitch rides?

It's usually people that hitch rides in cars, but sometimes cars themselves get taken for a ride. It happens when new cars are carried on trucks or trains from the factories where they are made, to showrooms where they are sold.

● It may sometimes look as if cars are about to roll off transporters, but don't worry – they're tied firmly in place.

What are houses made from?

Most houses are made from bricks, but they can be built out of almost anything – as long as it's strong and it keeps out the weather. Builders like to use materials they can get hold of easily – bricks or stone, wood, reeds, or mud.

• Bricklayers put mortar between the bricks. Mortar is a mixture of water, sand and cement, and it glues the bricks together.

• Houses protect us from the heat in summer, and the cold and rain in winter.

• There are about 12,000 bricks in the outside walls of a two-storey house.

● Some birds use mud to build their homes, but it's not shaped into little bricks!

● There aren't any bricks in the middle of a forest, but there's plenty of wood for building cabins.

● In the marshes of southern Iraq, in the Middle East, people use bundles of river reeds to build beautiful homes.

● In hot places such as Africa, people often build with mud and straw. The mixture dries hard in the sunshine.

113

What holds up the ceiling?

The weight of ceilings and floors is carried by strong wooden beams called joists. There are joists hidden away under the floorboards and above the ceiling of every room.

● The roof is held up by thick wooden rafters. Tiles keep out the rain.

Rafter

Joist

● Sometimes uninvited visitors live under the floor, such as the wood-eating grubs of the woodworm beetle.

114

What's behind the walls?

Among other things, there's usually
a lot of air! That's because most brick
houses have double outer walls, with a gap
between the walls. Pipes and electrical wiring
are tucked away in this gap.

● Building a house is teamwork.
A plumber lays all the pipes, an
electrician does the wiring, and
a carpenter puts in the windows,
doors and cupboards.

What's under the floor?

There are pipes under the floor. Some
carry clean water around the house.
Others take dirty water away. Some
aren't for water at all – they carry
gas, which is burned to heat ovens for
cooking and water for washing.

Why do houses need holes?

Most houses start with holes in the ground. The holes are filled with runny concrete, which hardens as it sets. The rest of the house is then built on top of this firm base, called the foundations.

• Many diggers have a wide front bucket, as well as the digging bucket at the back.

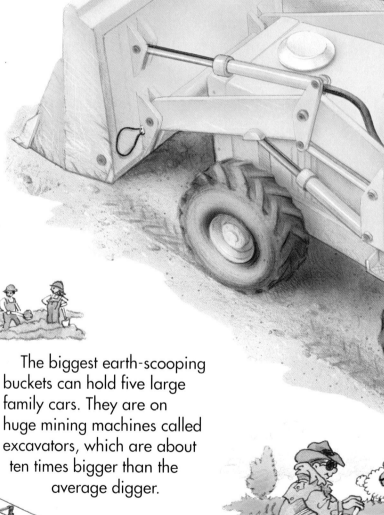

• A digger can dig a trench as fast as 20 people with spades.

The biggest earth-scooping buckets can hold five large family cars. They are on huge mining machines called excavators, which are about ten times bigger than the average digger.

• Diggers also dig holes for swimming pools, rubbish heaps and top-secret underground hiding places!

What do diggers do?

A digger does much more than dig.
Its wide front bucket is brilliant at
scooping rubble into a truck.
A scissor-like bucket
can also be fitted to the
front, to grab and lift
logs and pipes.

● A huge hammer can be
fitted to a digger, allowing
it to smash up rocks.

Do buildings have roots?

Skyscraper foundations are called piles and they are made of steel or concrete. Piles do the same job for a skyscraper as roots do for a tree. They stop it blowing over in the wind, or sinking into the ground under its own weight.

Which are the world's biggest hammers?

To knock a nail into wood, you use a hammer. To drive a steel pile into the ground, builders use a huge hammer called a piledriver. A crane lifts up the piledriver, then drops it on to the pile with a deafening BANG!

Which are the world's largest corkscrews?

Sometimes, the holes for piles are drilled with an auger – a long tool which works like a giant corkscrew, twisting its way deep down into the ground. A steel rod is put into the hole, and then lots of concrete is poured down around it.

● The piles for some skyscrapers are well over 50 metres deep. That's the same as five houses buried one on top of one another!

● Using piledrivers at night is against the law in many towns and cities. They're much too noisy.

Do buildings have a skeleton?

Nowadays, most big buildings have a strong steel framework inside them. This framework does a similar job to the bony skeleton inside your body. It props up the building and stops it from collapsing to the ground.

● Some beams are joined by big nails called rivets. These are punched through holes. Then their ends are flattened to stop them slipping out again.

● Other beams are joined by welding. The ends are heated until they melt and flow together like runny chocolate. When they cool down, the joined ends have hardened together.

● A skyscraper's framework is made from steel beams and tubes. The ends of one kind of beam look like the letters I or H. Beams this shape are stronger and lighter than square beams.

Do buildings have a skin?

The skin of a building is formed by its windows and walls. On modern skyscrapers these are made of glass or plastic panels, and thin concrete or stone sheets. These panels and sheets are called cladding.

Why are some buildings knocked down?

Buildings are knocked down when they are so old or damaged that they're unsafe. Or when someone wants to put a bigger, better building in their place. The quickest way to destroy them is to blow them up with explosives.

● It only takes a few seconds to blow a building up, but it takes a lot longer to work out how to do it safely! Experts decide how much explosive to use, and where to place it.

How do you wreck a building?

You smash it to pieces by swinging a huge metal wrecking ball from a crane! At 10 tonnes, a big wrecking ball weighs as much as 14 cars, and can do a lot of damage as it bashes into a wall.

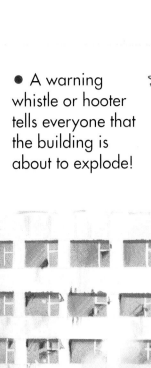

● A warning whistle or hooter tells everyone that the building is about to explode!

● Canadian karate experts once knocked down a seven-roomed farmhouse with their bare hands and feet in just over 3 hours.

How do you clear up all the mess?

Bulldozers start, by pushing all the rubble into big heaps. Then diggers scoop it up and load it in dump trucks. The trucks drive off to a special rubbish tip and dump their loads. Then they return to the building site for more.

Which are the world's tallest buildings?

Skyscrapers are the world's tallest buildings – but they've only held the record for 100 years or so. Before then, the world's tallest buildings were the great cathedrals of Europe.

3 The Eiffel Tower, Paris, France, 300 m high, built in 1887-89.

● In some skyscrapers, people live high above the clouds. They have to phone down to find out if it's raining at street level!

1 The Great Pyramid was built 4,500 years ago at Giza, in Egypt. It's 146 m high.

2 Before its spire fell down in 1548, England's Lincoln Cathedral topped 160 m.

● The world's tallest house of cards was well over 4 metres high – that's nearly twice as high as your bedroom ceiling.

4 The Empire State Building, New York, USA, 381 m high, built in 1929-30.

5 The world's tallest building, the Sears Tower, Chicago, USA, 443 m high, built in 1970-73.

● No one likes climbing stairs, so it's a good thing passenger lifts were invented in the 1850s.

When was the first skyscraper built?

In 1885, the people of Chicago, USA, were amazed to see a ten-storey building being built in their city. It was the world's first skyscraper. Over the next 15 years, the cities of Chicago and New York raced each other to build the world's tallest skyscraper.

Which roof opens when the Sun shines?

The SkyDome sports stadium in Toronto, Canada, has a roof which can open and close. Three gigantic steel panels slide back in good weather to make the stadium open-air. If it starts to rain, the roof closes again – but it takes 20 minutes, so don't forget your umbrella!

● Seafood is so popular in Japan that there's even a fish-shaped restaurant. It's in a large seaport called Kobe.

Which building is inside out?

The outside of the Pompidou Centre in Paris is covered in things that are normally hidden away inside. There are lifts, stairs, water pipes, electricity cables – even toilets. It's rather like having your lungs, muscles and veins on the outside of your body!

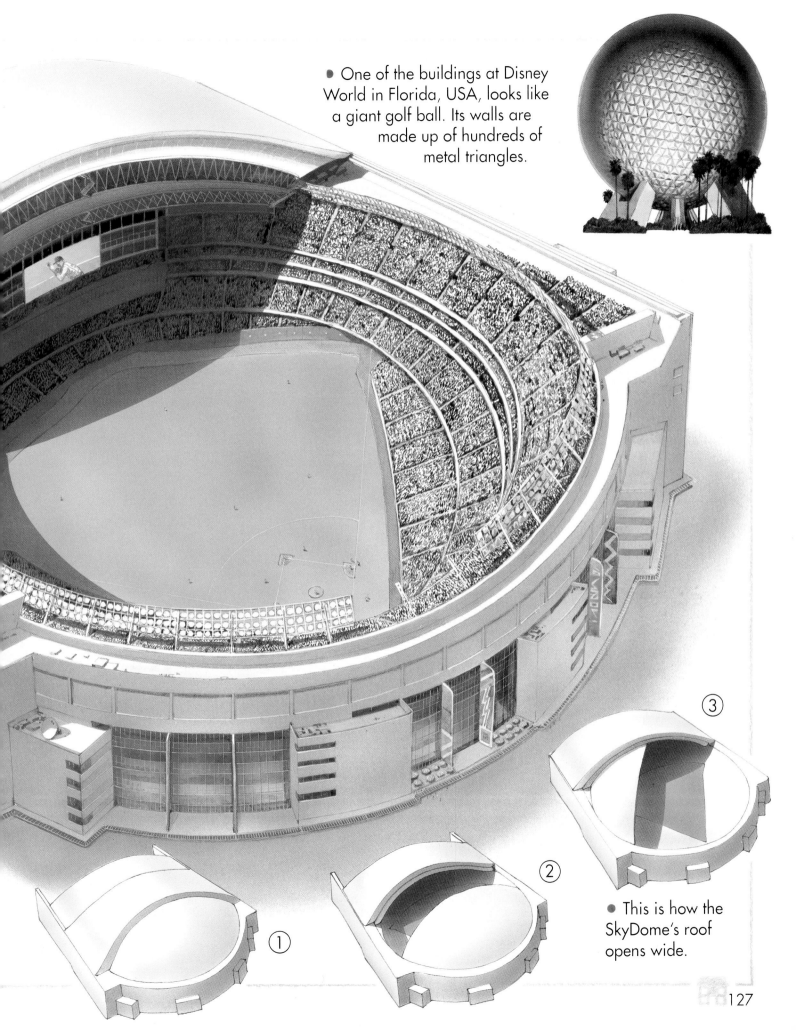

● One of the buildings at Disney World in Florida, USA, looks like a giant golf ball. Its walls are made up of hundreds of metal triangles.

①

②

③

● This is how the SkyDome's roof opens wide.

Why are tunnels round?

Tunnels are round because drills make round holes! Even tunnels dug with spades have arched roofs. That's because an arch is a much stronger shape than a square. Big tunnels are carved out by tunnel-boring machines (TBMs, for short). These are like gigantic drills, twisting and grinding their way through the ground.

● The Eurotunnel TBM's cutting head has over 100 cutting rollers and 200 sharp gnashing teeth.

● The Eurotunnel between Britain and France is 50 kilometres long. If all the earth and rock from the tunnel were piled up, it would be as tall as the Eiffel Tower.

How do you tunnel through hard rock?

Even the most powerful TBM can't cope with really hard rock. Tunnel-builders have to use explosives to blast their way, a little bit at a time.

● Tunnels aren't just for big things like cars and trains. Smaller tunnels carry electricity cables, as well as gas, water and sewage pipes.

Can a mole dig as fast as a TBM?

A mole can dig five times faster than a TBM, using nothing but its two front paws. It's a lot smaller, though, and so are its tunnels!

You can probably guess what the TBM's nickname is – the mole, of course!

How are bridges built?

Like buildings, bridges start with deep foundation holes. These are filled with metal and concrete, then towers called piers are built on top. The deck is often made from sections, hoisted into place by cranes. Finally, the road or railway is laid on top of the deck.

● Deck sections are brought to the site on barges, towed by tugboats.

● It takes a team of 29 painters three years to paint Scotland's 521-metre-long Forth Railway Bridge. When they finish, they have to start all over again!

Deck

Pier

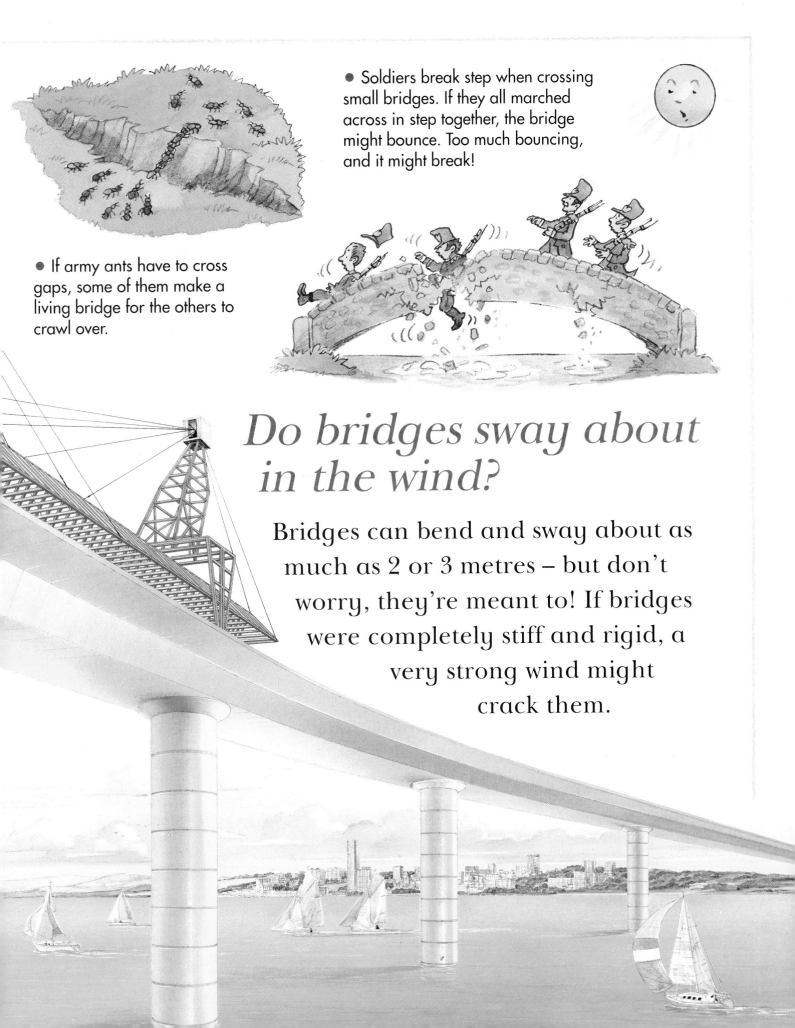

• If army ants have to cross gaps, some of them make a living bridge for the others to crawl over.

• Soldiers break step when crossing small bridges. If they all marched across in step together, the bridge might bounce. Too much bouncing, and it might break!

Do bridges sway about in the wind?

Bridges can bend and sway about as much as 2 or 3 metres – but don't worry, they're meant to! If bridges were completely stiff and rigid, a very strong wind might crack them.

Which bridge can break in two?

London's Tower Bridge carries traffic over the river Thames. The roadway is built in two halves, which can be raised or lowered like drawbridges. When a tall ship sails up the river, each half of the bridge lifts up so that the ship can pass through.

● Bungee-jumpers love the Royal Gorge Bridge in Colorado, USA. At 321 metres above the surface of the river, it's the highest bridge in the world.

● Tower Bridge isn't named for its tall towers, but after its neighbour, the Tower of London.

INVENTIONS

Why do people invent things?

Inventors try to solve problems. They think about people's needs, and come up with an answer. When an inventor noticed how inconvenient big umbrellas were, he invented a folding one that would fit in a bag.

Gone to buy some glue!

● Post-it notes were invented by accident when someone made a glue that didn't stick properly. You could stick down a piece of paper, peel it off, and then re-stick it!

● From the moment you wake up you're surrounded by inventions. Pillows, light bulbs, and even cornflakes all help to give us an easier, comfier life.

● Some inventions are just for fun. The first Frisbees were empty pie tins belonging to a baker called Joseph Frisbie. When some of his customers tossed the tins to each other in the park, the idea for the Frisbee was born.

• Safety pins were introduced almost 200 years ago, but have a much longer history. Their inventor copied the idea from clasps worn by the Ancient Egyptians.

Is everything invented?

No it isn't! An invention is something new like a paper-clip, which never existed before someone thought of it. But things like coal and rubber weren't invented. They were already in the world, and just had to be discovered.

• When people first discovered the milky juice of the rubber tree they used it to make rubber. Later, someone invented rubber tyres for cars and bicycles.

Where do inventors get their ideas?

Inventors get ideas for their inventions in lots of different places. Some of them study plants and animals to see how they have solved their problems. Others look at ideas from other places or from the past. Very few ideas come out of the blue.

• Burdock seeds are covered with tiny hooks that stick to things, but can be pulled off. An engineer who noticed this used his discovery to make Velcro for fastenings.

Which calendar was carved in stone?

Many hundreds of years ago, people called the Aztecs lived in Central America. They made a calendar from a huge stone shaped like the Sun. The face of the Sun god was carved in the middle, and signs for the days were carved all around the edge.

Who invented our calendar?

More than 2,000 years ago a Roman ruler called Julius Caesar invented the calendar we use today. He gave each year 365 days, and arranged them in 12 months. Since then, the calendar has hardly changed.

- The Aztec calendar stone measured nearly 4 metres from side to side – that's far too big to hang on the wall!

What is a leap year?

Every four years we have what we call a leap year. This is a year with 366 days instead of 365. The extra day is added to the end of February. So if your birthday falls on February 29th, it's a very special day indeed.

- A leap year can always be divided by four with none left over. The years 1996, 2000 and 2004 are all leap years.

Why do we need calendars?

Most of us need calendars to help us remember all the things we plan in a year. But they also help us keep track of time. When people are shipwrecked or taken hostage, they find unusual ways to mark the passing days.

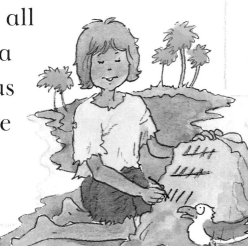

Why does my watch tick?

More than 20 tiny wheels are packed neatly inside your watch. You can hear them tick and tock as the teeth of one wheel lock into the teeth of the next. The moving wheels keep time, and slowly turn the hands around the watch face.

How did people manage before clocks?

Before clocks were invented, people judged the time by looking at the Sun. They got up at sunrise, and went to bed when it was dark. They ate lunch when the Sun was up above, and ate dinner when it set in the west.

● Sailors usually work for four hours at a time. Bells ring every half an hour – one after half an hour, two after an hour and so on. When eight bells sound, the shift is over, and the sailors can take a well-earned rest.

How does a grandfather keep good time?

A tall grandfather clock has a long pendulum that swings back and forth in a steady rhythm. With every swing, wheels inside the clock slowly turn, moving the hands round the face. Winding the clock with a key stops it slowing down.

● Sundials are one of the oldest kinds of clock. Instead of a moving hand, they have a shadow, cast by the Sun. As the Earth turns during the day, the 'hand' moves around the clock.

How can you split a second?

Today's electronic timers are so accurate that they can split a second into a million parts. In competitions, athletes are timed to a hundredth of a second – that's less than the time it takes for you to blink.

Which timer was a load of old rope?

About 400 years ago a ship's speed was measured with a log tied to a knotted rope. The sailors threw the log overboard, and counted how many knots unwound as the ship moved forward. They used a sandglass to time it accurately. Sailors still measure a ship's speed in knots today. One knot is just under two kilometres an hour.

● Musicians use noisy clicking timers called metronomes to help them keep in time. Orchestras don't – they have a silent waving conductor!

How can you cook an egg with sand?

Four minutes is all it takes for the sand inside an egg-timer to run from the top to the bottom. And that's just the right time to boil an egg. Sandglasses are simple and accurate, and have been used for hundreds of years. Once the timer has finished, you just turn it upside down to start again!

● Cyclists fix speedometers to the wheels of their bikes to measure how fast they're cycling.

How did a till settle a row?

In James Ritty's saloon in Ohio, USA, the customers were always arguing with the staff about how much they had to pay for their drinks. So in 1879 Ritty invented a cash register, which rang up the prices, kept a record of how much money was in the till, and gave Ritty and his staff a much more peaceful life.

● Since 1980, goods sold in shops have had a bar code on them. Only a laser scanner can understand the bar code's pattern, which contains all sorts of information about the item.

Who used tea as money?

People in Tibet and China once used tea pressed into blocks as money. Before coins were invented, people used to swap things like shells, beads or grain for the goods they wanted.

● The Chinese first used paper bank-notes about 1,200 years ago. They printed some of their notes on the bark of the mulberry tree.

How can a supermarket trolley make you rich?

The person who invented the world's first supermarket trolley became a millionaire. Sylvan Goldman's trolley was little more than a chair on wheels, with two baskets fitted on the top, but it earned him a fortune.

● Inventions needn't be grand. When Margaret Knight invented flat-bottomed paper bags, she became a wealthy woman. The bags held twice as much shopping!

What did people use before fridges?

Electric fridges were invented around 1920. Before then, people kept their food in a wooden cupboard called an icebox. Huge blocks from the ice man kept the cupboard cold.

● Coca-Cola didn't start out as a fizzy drink. An American chemist called John Pemberton invented it as a sweet syrup in 1885. Soda water was added to it later.

Who ate the first cornflakes?

Two brothers, Will and John Kellogg, invented cornflakes by accident, when they were trying to make a new type of bread. One day, they overcooked a pan of wheat, rolled the mixture flat, and then watched it dry into flakes. They toasted the flakes and tasted them – delicious!

● The ice man called several times a week to deliver large blocks of ice for the icebox.

● Long ago, people made natural fridges by lining caves and holes with a thick layer of snow in winter. These ice houses kept fresh food cool right through the warm summer months.

● In 1853, a new food was invented. When a diner asked for extra-thin chips, the chef came up with the first potato crisps.

How were drinking straws invented?

One hot summer in the 1880s, a man called Marvin Stone made the first paper straw. He'd noticed that people kept drinks cooler by not touching the glass and using a hollow grass stalk to suck up the liquid.

How do you make toast without a toaster?

People made toast long before there were electric toasters. They put a piece of bread on the end of a long toasting fork, and held it in front of a fire. Unfortunately, the bread burnt easily, and needed very careful watching. The first pop-up toaster was invented in the USA about 70 years ago.

• Electric toasters save us from having to keep an eye on the toast – and from burning it, too!

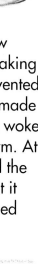

• In 1937 a new automatic tea-making machine was invented. It heated water, made the tea and then woke you with an alarm. At first it was called the Cheerywake, but it was soon renamed the Teasmade.

Who invented the microwave oven?

Percy Spencer invented the microwave oven just after the Second World War. He'd been working on ways of using invisible waves to detect enemy planes. When the waves melted the chocolate bar in his pocket, he realized they'd be useful for cooking too!

● Microwaves are invisible waves of energy. When they're beamed at food, any water in the food starts to shake violently, and gets very hot. The heat passes quickly through the food, and cooks it all the way through.

● About 100 years ago, only rich people had electricity in their homes. The first electrical gadgets were dangerous things, and servants sometimes risked their lives by using them.

Why don't non-stick frying pans stick?

Non-stick pans don't stick because they are coated with something as slippery as ice, called Teflon. Teflon is actually a kind of plastic, and was invented in the late 1930s. But it took years for someone to come up with the idea of sticking the stuff on to a pan!

Who first flushed the toilet?

Four hundred years ago Sir John Harrington built a flushing toilet for his godmother, Queen Elizabeth I. In those days very few homes had water pipes or drains, so ordinary people had to carry on using their chamber pots.

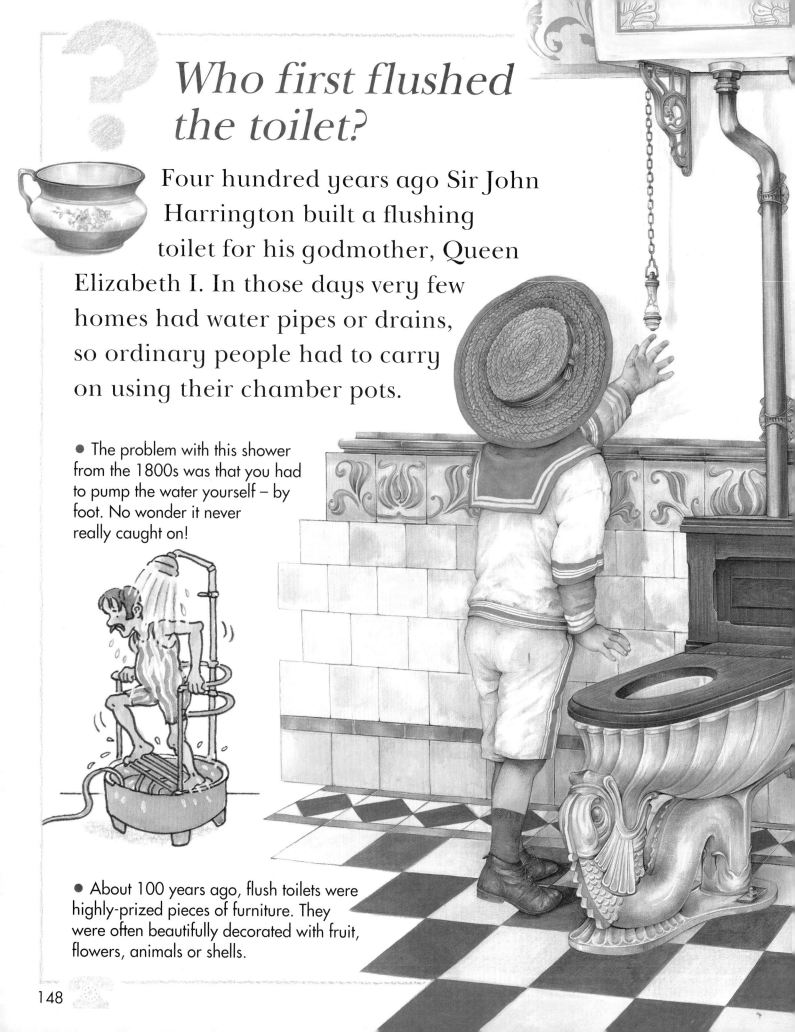

● The problem with this shower from the 1800s was that you had to pump the water yourself – by foot. No wonder it never really caught on!

● About 100 years ago, flush toilets were highly-prized pieces of furniture. They were often beautifully decorated with fruit, flowers, animals or shells.

Who first jumped in the bath?

The people of Greece, Rome and the Indus Valley in Pakistan all enjoyed a bath in ancient times. But, as time went by, baths went out of fashion and many people never even washed. They used perfumes to cover up the pong!

● The Chinese used pig's hair to make the first toothbrushes about 500 years ago. Luckily for pigs, nylon brushes came along in the 1930s!

How did horses help keep carpets clean?

The first carpet-cleaning machine was towed by horses! It was parked outside the house because of its smelly petrol engine. Long pipes stretched through the windows and sucked up all the dirt. It was quite a sight and people often invited their friends round to watch!

Which came first – screws or screwdrivers?

Spiral or twisted nails were used in the 1500s in guns, armour and clocks. But, strangely, you couldn't unscrew a screw for another 300 years, when the handy screwdriver first appeared.

● Today's carpenters use many of the same tools as carpenters long ago.

● Screws weren't made by machine until the 1760s. The thread that runs round the screw had to be filed by hand. That must have been a fiddly task!

Who had everything under lock and key?

The Ancient Egyptians invented locks. Two wooden bolts fitted together snugly and were held in place by pins arranged in a pattern. The pins could only be freed with a key which had a matching pattern.

● With Gro-bags you can grow plants anywhere – even if you don't have a garden. These big bags of earth first appeared in 1973.

Could a horse mow the lawn?

The first lawnmowers were pulled by horses. The animals had to wear big rubber boots so they didn't leave messy hoof-prints all over the freshly-mown lawn!

● Lawnmower engines were used on the first go-karts. Today's Grand Prix champions probably all started out driving lawnmowers!

Which new invention was soon on everyone's lips?

In 1915 American scientists came up with a small invention that was a huge success. It was a creamy, colour crayon inside a case that could be wound up and used in a second – the very first lipstick.

● Ancient Egyptian women didn't have wind-up lipsticks, but they did colour their lips. They used golden clay mixed with juicy tree sap.

Who wore a mouthful of hippo teeth?

About 2,500 years ago people began to make false teeth from ivory or bone. Hippo bone was popular, but so was ox, cat and human bone. Unfortunately, all these false teeth soon turned brown and started to rot. They must have tasted dreadful!

• Before lipsticks, lip colours came in a pot. Many of them were waxes and ointments coloured with plant dyes such as grape juice.

• A French hairdresser has used a video camera linked to a computer to show his clients what they would look like with different styles – short hair, long hair, or no hair at all!

Why were plasters first invented?

Earl Dickson invented plasters for his wife, who kept cutting herself in the kitchen. He stuck small squares of cloth on to pieces of sticky tape, covering them carefully to stop the glue drying out. Whenever his wife cut herself, she just grabbed a piece of the tape, and stuck it on.

• Before Mr King Camp Gillette invented safe, modern razors in 1895, men shaved with sharp cut-throat razors – and hoped that their hand wouldn't slip!

153

Who invented raincoats?

The first waterproof raincoats were made in 1823 by Charles Macintosh – which is why they are often called macs. He made the cloth waterproof by sandwiching a layer of rubber between two lengths of cotton. The coats kept people dry all right, but they weighed a ton and smelt awful when they got wet!

● A lot of today's rainwear is made of PVC. It's a plastic-backed material which comes in lots of bright colours.

● It rains so much in Scotland that hill farmers buy raincoats for their sheep!

Why do zips have teeth?

Without their teeth, zips couldn't open or close. The two rows of teeth are joined by a slider, which locks them together or pulls them apart. Zips were invented in the 1890s, and were a great improvement on fiddly buttons and hooks and eyes.

• The first jeans were made by Levi Strauss for gold miners in the USA. He made them in a hard-wearing blue cloth that was used to make tents. These days it's better known as denim.

Can clothes keep you feeling fit?

Some clothes can do amazing things. You can even buy tights full of health-giving vitamins, which are usually only found in fresh fruit and veg!

• When Thomas Hancock invented elastic in 1820, he thought it would be useful along the top of pockets to stop thieves. It was someone else who realized it would be just right for holding up people's underwear!

Who scored goals in a basket?

The very first basketball players used two old peach baskets as goals. Basketball was invented about 100 years ago by coach James Naismith, who was looking for an exciting game to play indoors on cold winter nights.

Why are trainers so springy?

Trainers have springy soles made of rubber and little pockets of air. Each time you take a step, the rubber gets squashed down, but quickly springs back to its original size. All this squashing and springing makes your feet bounce off the ground, and helps you to run a little bit faster.

● Early basketball players had to climb a ladder to get the ball back after a goal. Things are easier today – now the goal nets have a hole in the bottom.

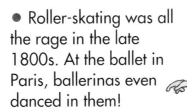

● Roller-skating was all the rage in the late 1800s. At the ballet in Paris, ballerinas even danced in them!

How did people ice-skate in summer?

Before there were ice rinks, people could only ice-skate outdoors in the winter. Then someone came up with the idea of making a 'ground' skate that people could enjoy in the summer, too. Instead of a blade, they put wheels on the sole and hey presto – the roller skate had arrived!

● Jet-skis first went on sale in Japan in 1979. Jet-skiers have to steer well clear of bathers. The very latest models can zoom along at speeds of 105 km/h.

Why are bears called teddies?

Teddy bears are named after the American President, Theodore Roosevelt, who was called Teddy for short. Once, on a hunting trip, he came across a bear cub and refused to shoot it. A sweetshop owner who read about the story in the paper decided to give up his shop and make toy bears. He called them teddies, after the President.

● The construction toys Meccano and Lego were both invented to encourage children to build things, not destroy them! You can use them to make all sorts of inventions!

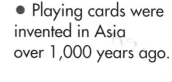

● Playing cards were invented in Asia over 1,000 years ago.

158

Which toy is 6,000 years old?

Dolls are probably the oldest toys of all. Roman children played with dolls made of rags. Dolls have been made from all sorts of materials – wood, wax, paper, china and plastic.

● Barbie went on sale in 1959. She was the first-ever doll to have a grown-up's body.

When did home computer games appear?

The first home computer games appeared in 1974. Compared to today's games, they weren't very exciting. There were no life-and-death battles in outer space – you hit a ball to and fro with a bat!

What were the first cars like?

The first cars were steam engines on wheels – noisy, smoky machines that scared other road-users! But these steam cars soon got quicker and easier to drive. They were used for nearly 30 years, until they were replaced by faster cars with petrol engines.

● In the 1930s, planes carried 20 passengers at the most. By the 1970s, the new jumbo jets could seat up to 500! Soon, new super-jumbos will carry as many as 850 people!

How do you ride on air?

People ride on air every time they travel on a hovercraft. The hovercraft was invented by Christopher Cockerell in 1959. He discovered that trapping a cushion of air beneath a boat lifts it up above the waves, allowing it to travel much faster.

• The penny-farthing bicycle was invented in the 1860s. It had two wheels – one very large and one very small – and was named after two British coins of the time – the large penny and the tiny farthing.

• Eveyone knows about seat belts for people to wear, but did you know that cats and dogs can wear them too? So clunk-click, Rover/Felix!

• The first cars weren't allowed to go faster than 3 km/h. And someone had to walk in front with a flag to warn other road-users!

Which bikes have sails?

The fastest superbikes have solid wheels and flat frames that work in the same way as a sail. As the bike zooms along, its wheels and frame catch the wind, which helps to push the bike forward – just as it does on a boat. But most of the power still comes from turning the pedals!

Who cycled over the sea?

In June 1979, American Bryan Allen pedalled a special plane called the *Gossamer Albatross* across the Channel, from England to France, in just under 2 hours and 50 minutes.

Nine years later, Kanellos Kanellopoulos of Greece pedalled his *Daedalus 88* over the sea between the islands of Crete and Santorini.

Can bikes climb mountains?

Machines called mountain bikes are specially designed for rough stony ground. Their frames are extra-strong so they can stand up to rattling over bumps, while their knobbly tyres grip well even in slippery sand or mud.

● It's not easy to balance on a unicycle – it only has one wheel!

● When the first bicycles were invented, about 200 years ago, they didn't have any pedals! People rolled them along by pushing against the ground with their feet.

How many people can ride on a bike?

Although most bikes are designed for one rider, special bikes are sometimes built to take more. The world's longest bike was built in Belgium. It had seats and pedals for 35 people, but it was very difficult for them to all balance and cycle at once!

How can you fit 1,000 books in your pocket?

There's room for about 1,000 storybooks on a CD-ROM – a small compact disc that's as thin as your fingernail and can fit in a pocket. Words, pictures and sounds can all be stored on CD-ROMs, but they only work with a computer, so you can't read one on the bus – yet!

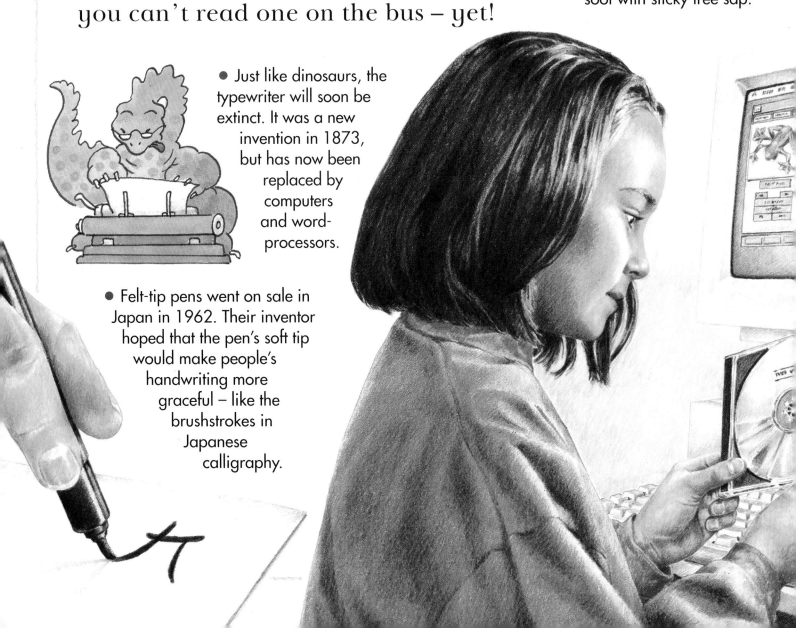

● The Egyptians were one of the first peoples to write with ink. They made it by mixing black soot with sticky tree sap.

● Just like dinosaurs, the typewriter will soon be extinct. It was a new invention in 1873, but has now been replaced by computers and word-processors.

● Felt-tip pens went on sale in Japan in 1962. Their inventor hoped that the pen's soft tip would make people's handwriting more graceful – like the brushstrokes in Japanese calligraphy.

● Today's pocket calculators can carry out calculations much quicker than you can move your fingers. They are as powerful as the huge computers of the 1960s.

Which computer was as big as a bus?

The first computer was about as long as four buses and was called Colossus. It was built in Britain and was switched on in 1943. Very few people knew about it at the time, because one of its first jobs was to crack secret codes in the war.

Who was Mr Biro?

Ladislao Biro invented the ballpoint pen in 1938. It contained a tube of long-lasting, quick-drying ink, which rolled evenly onto the paper thanks to a tiny ball at the tip. Although Biro called his pen a ballpoint, most people now call their ballpoint a biro!

Who took hours to take a photo?

A Frenchman called Joseph Niépce took the first-ever photograph in 1826. He had to wait eight hours before the picture was captured on a thin metal plate coated with a sort of tar. The photo was of the view from his window.

● Niépce would have found it hard to believe, but today's Polaroid cameras can produce a picture in seconds!

● In the late 1800s, it took so long to take a photo that sitters needed a back-rest to help them sit still!

When could you watch pink TV?

The first TV had an odd picture – bright pink and very fuzzy! But its inventor, John Logie Baird, had used very odd equipment to build it, including a bicycle light and a knitting needle!

● The world's smallest radio is about the size of a pea!

Who invented the personal stereo?

A Walkman is a personal cassette player with headphones, which is light enough to carry around. It was invented in 1979 by a Japanese electrical company called Sony.

● The first telephone service started in 1878, in a small town in the USA. Only 20 people had phones, so they could only ring up each other!

Why does the telephone ring?

The telephone rings to let you know that someone wants to speak to you! So if your friend dials your number, your phone rings out. When you answer, an electric current carries your voice along the line and your friend hears you loud and clear!

• Today, most telephone exchanges connect calls automatically with computers.

• Telephone calls used to be connected by hand. An operator asked which telephone number you wanted and plugged in the correct wire.

How can glass link the world?

Optical fibres are hair-thin strands of glass, twisted into cable. They have been laid under all the oceans and act as highways for anything from phone calls to TV programmes. Information travels along them at the speed of light.

● Telephones come in all shapes and sizes, from tiny mobiles to cartoon characters. But they all have two main parts – the transmitter you talk into and the receiver which you listen to.

Are phone lines just for voices?

Voices aren't the only things that travel along a phone line. With a videophone, you can see a picture of who's telephoning as well. With a fax, you can send letters, photos and drawings. And computers use phone lines to communicate with one another too!

● There are over 100 million telephones in the United States. In Washington DC, there are more phones than people!

Can a robot play the piano?

A clever Japanese robot called WABOT-2 can whizz its fingers over a keyboard much faster than a human can. It can either read new music, or choose a song it has played before and stored in its memory. The cleverest thing about WABOT-2 is its sensitive fingers. It can play gently or furiously.

● WABOT-2's head is like a camcorder. As the robot reads music, the camera 'films' what it sees and stores it in its memory to play again.

WABOT - 2

Where do people mix music?

In a recording studio, the voices and instruments are recorded separately. The producer mixes the parts together on a machine called a mixing desk. He or she checks the sounds are balanced and every part can be heard clearly.

● Drum machines make the sound of all sorts of drums – but they're only as big as a chocolate box. Some of them have pads to tap out your rhythm on.

● You can record any sound you like on a sampler – even a dog's bark. You put the sounds you've sampled into tunes as if they were musical notes.

Can you be an entire orchestra?

Synthesisers are machines that can make the sound of every instrument in the orchestra. One minute they sound like a flute, the next they sound like a violin. They'll even play a simple drum pattern to give your music a beat.

How can you fight a hungry dinosaur?

When you put on a virtual reality helmet, you enter an imaginary world. You could be fighting a man-eating dinosaur or visiting aliens in space. Everything inside the helmet looks and sounds real, but is actually created by a computer.

● As you press buttons in the special data-glove, the computer changes the pictures you see and the sounds you hear.

● Anyone can be an inventor! What would you like to invent?

HISTORY

How long ago did dinosaurs live?

Dinosaurs lived millions of years ago. The first ones lived about 230 million years ago, and the last ones we know about died out over 65 million years ago. Compared to this, human history is just a hiccup – we've only been around for the last 2 million years!

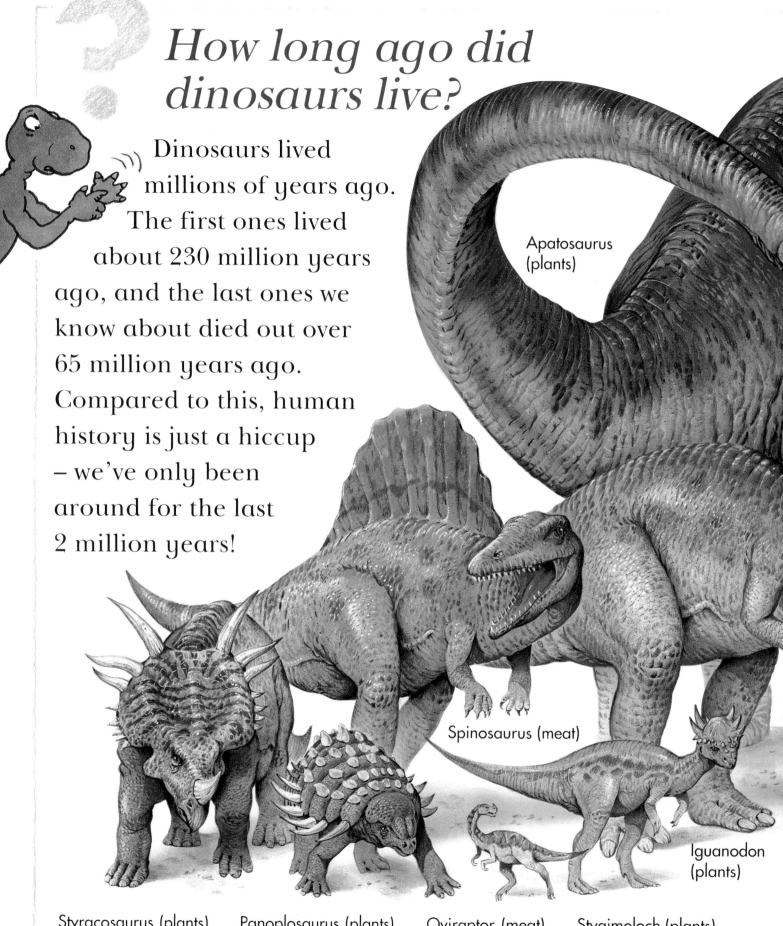

Apatosaurus (plants)

Spinosaurus (meat)

Iguanodon (plants)

Styracosaurus (plants) Panoplosaurus (plants) Oviraptor (meat) Stygimoloch (plants)

● Dinosaurs were reptiles. Today's reptiles include lizards, crocodiles, tortoises and snakes.

● Like most other reptiles, dinosaurs lived on land and had dry scaly skin. Their eggs had leathery shells, unlike birds' eggs which are hard and brittle.

How many dinosaurs were there?

There were lots of different dinosaurs. Scientists have already named about 300 kinds, and new ones are being found all the time. Some dinosaurs were big, others were tiny. Some were fierce meat-eaters, others were gentle vegetarians which browsed on juicy plants.

● Dinosaurs ruled the Earth for a mind-boggling 165 million years!

Kentrosaurus (plants)

How are dinosaur fossils found?

Dinosaur fossils are usually buried inside rock, so they have to be dug out. People sometimes stumble across them by accident, but most fossils are found by scientists who go looking in likely places. This is easier than it sounds, because only some kinds of rock have dinosaur fossils in them.

● One of the first jobs is to make a map of the digging area. Then, each time a fossil is found, it can be marked on the map.

● Fossils are usually found in sandstone, clay, limestone or shale rocks.

● It may take weeks, months, or even years to dig out a whole skeleton.

● Dinosaurs are sometimes named after the person who found them.

● Photographs show exactly how a piece of bone was lying. This can help the scientists when they put the skeleton together again.

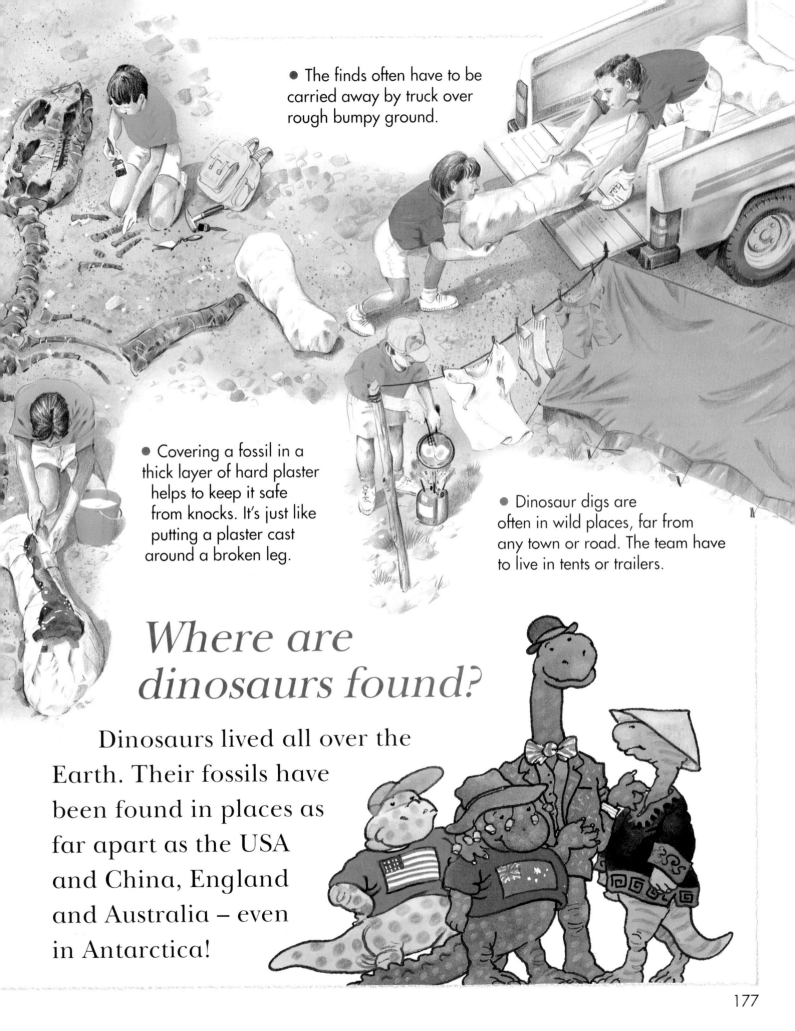

● The finds often have to be carried away by truck over rough bumpy ground.

● Covering a fossil in a thick layer of hard plaster helps to keep it safe from knocks. It's just like putting a plaster cast around a broken leg.

● Dinosaur digs are often in wild places, far from any town or road. The team have to live in tents or trailers.

Where are dinosaurs found?

Dinosaurs lived all over the Earth. Their fossils have been found in places as far apart as the USA and China, England and Australia – even in Antarctica!

What happened to the dinosaurs?

Something very strange happened 65 million years ago. All the dinosaurs vanished, together with all the flying reptiles and most of the sea reptiles. No one knows for sure what happened to them.

● Many scientists think giant rocks from outer space smashed into the Earth, throwing up great clouds of dust which blotted out the Sun. This changed the weather and killed off most plants. First the plant-eating dinosaurs died of cold and hunger, then the meat-eaters.

● Perhaps the dinosaurs were poisoned by new kinds of plants.

● A few people believe that sea reptiles like Elasmosaurus didn't die out, and that families of them now live in big lakes like Scotland's Loch Ness!

● Archaeopteryx looked like a dinosaur with feathers, but it wasn't. It lived 140 million years ago, and it is the oldest bird we know about. It was a very strange bird, though, because it had a tail, clawed fingers and teeth, just like a dinosaur.

Are there any dinosaurs around today?

Although there aren't any true dinosaurs alive today, we do have some of their relatives. Scientists think that birds developed from dinosaurs, because their skeletons are so similar. So look carefully the next time you see a bird nesting in a tree or hopping across the grass!

179

Why do we call Egyptians ancient?

We call the Egyptians ancient because they lived such a long time ago – not because they all reached a ripe old age! The first Egyptians were farmers about 8,000 years ago. Within a few thousand years, Egypt had become one of the most powerful countries in the world.

● Will people be studying us in 5,000 years' time? What will they think about the way we live now?

● The Egyptians usually built tombs for dead kings on the river's western bank, where the Sun sets. They believed that their kings went to meet the Sun god when they died.

● Egypt is mostly sandy desert, where nothing grows. The Ancient Egyptians settled on the banks of the river Nile, where there was plenty of water for themselves and their crops.

• The Ancient Egyptians didn't know about distant parts of the world. But they did explore parts of Asia and Africa. And their merchants bought wood, gold, ivory, spices and even apes from nearby countries.

Why were the Egyptians great?

The Egyptians were so good at farming that they became very rich. They built fantastic temples for their gods, and huge pointed tombs called pyramids where they buried their kings. They had armies and ships and courts of law. Their priests studied the stars and their craftspeople made beautiful things from gold and silver.

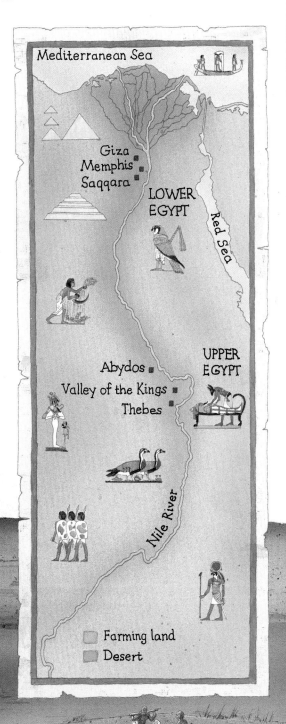

Mediterranean Sea

Giza
Memphis
Saqqara

LOWER
EGYPT

Red Sea

UPPER
EGYPT

Abydos
Valley of the Kings
Thebes

Nile River

☐ Farming land
☐ Desert

Who ruled Egypt?

The king of Egypt was called the pharaoh. The Egyptians believed that their Sun god Re was the first king of Egypt, and that all the pharaohs after him were his relatives. This made the pharaoh very holy – and very powerful! The people thought he was a god on Earth.

● The pharaoh's advisors were called the Honoured Ones. There were all sorts of royal officials, too, with grand names like the Director of Royal Dress and the Keeper of the Royal Wigs.

Could a woman be pharaoh?

Although very few women ruled Egypt, there was a famous pharaoh called Hatshepsut. When her six-year-old nephew came to the throne, Hatshepsut was asked to rule Egypt for him – just until he was a little bit older. But Hatshepsut liked ruling so much that she wouldn't let her nephew take over. He didn't get the chance to rule until he was 30 years old!

● When she was pharaoh, Hatshepsut had to wear the badges of royalty. These included a false beard, made of real hair.

How would you know if you met a pharaoh?

He would be wearing a crown, of course! In fact, pharaohs sometimes wore two crowns at the same time – a white one for Upper Egypt, which was the name for the south of the country, and a red one for Lower Egypt, which was the north.

Why did the Egyptians bury their mummies?

A mummy is a dead body which has been dried out so it lasts for thousands of years. The Egyptians believed that the dead travelled to another world, where they needed their bodies. And they didn't want any bits missing!

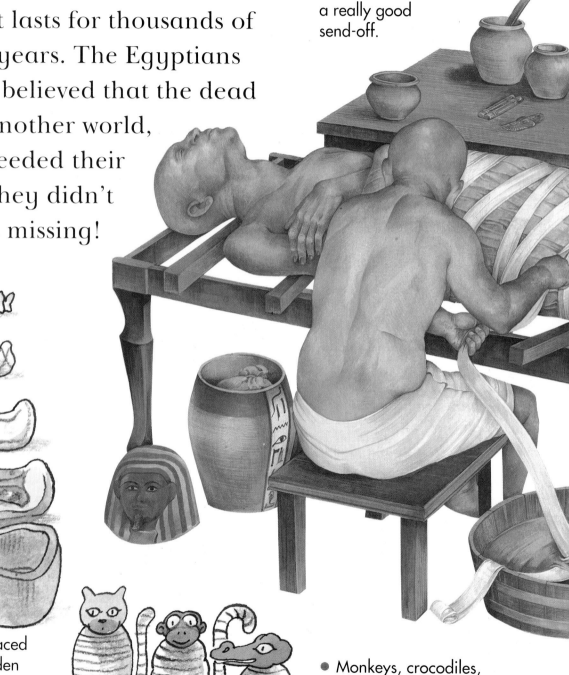

- Some poorer families had their nearest and dearest mummified, but it was an expensive business. Only the rich could afford a really good send-off.

- The mummy was placed inside a series of wooden coffins. These were put in a big stone case called a sarcophagus.

- Monkeys, crocodiles, cats and other sacred animals were often mummified, too!

Why were mummies brainless?

The Ancient Egyptians believed that the heart was the most important part of the whole body. They thought that the brain was useless. So when they were preparing a mummy, they took out the brain – by pulling it down through the nose!

Why were mummies wrapped in bandages?

Wrapping the dead body helped to keep its shape. After the insides were removed, the body was dried out for 40 days in salty stuff called natron. Then it was washed, rubbed with ointments, and tightly bandaged.

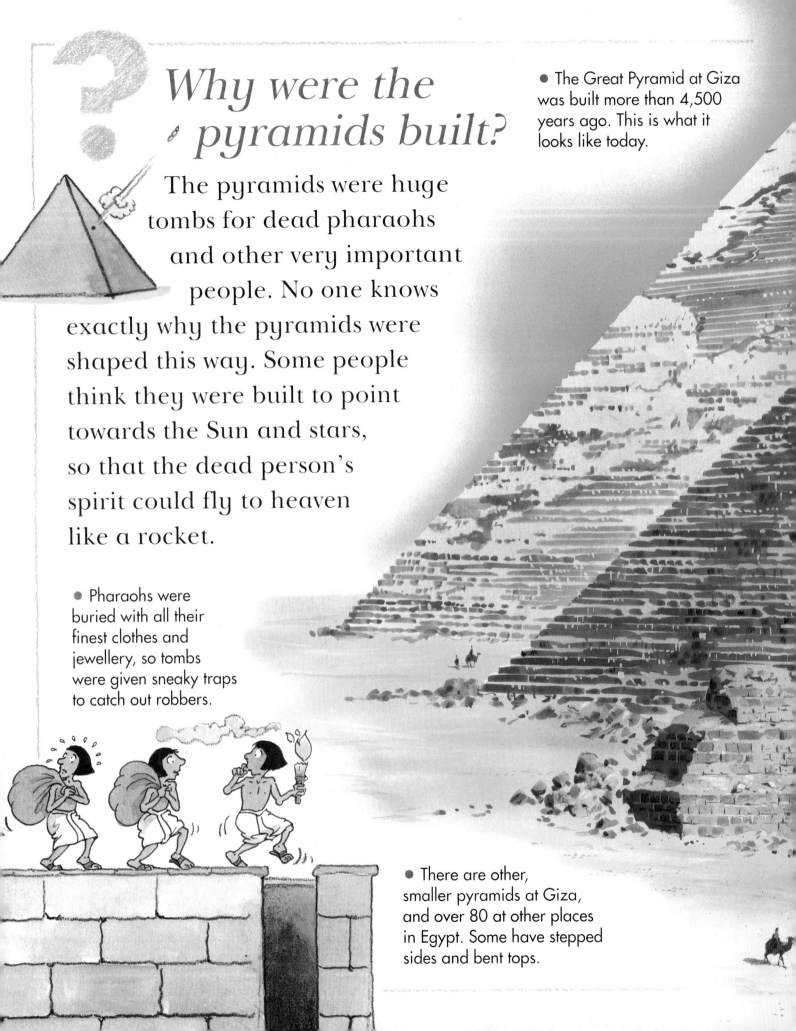

Why were the pyramids built?

The pyramids were huge tombs for dead pharaohs and other very important people. No one knows exactly why the pyramids were shaped this way. Some people think they were built to point towards the Sun and stars, so that the dead person's spirit could fly to heaven like a rocket.

● The Great Pyramid at Giza was built more than 4,500 years ago. This is what it looks like today.

● Pharaohs were buried with all their finest clothes and jewellery, so tombs were given sneaky traps to catch out robbers.

● There are other, smaller pyramids at Giza, and over 80 at other places in Egypt. Some have stepped sides and bent tops.

● This is what the
Great Pyramid
looks like
inside.

Pharaoh's
chamber

Who were the Ancient Greeks?

The Ancient Greeks were people who lived nearly 3,000 years ago. They didn't just live in Greece. Some of them lived to the north and the east, in lands that we now call Bulgaria and Turkey. Other Greeks lived on small rocky islands in the Mediterranean Sea.

● Many Greek people set sail for north Africa, Italy and France. They found safe harbours, where they built new homes and towns, and cleared the land for farming.

■ Greek Homeland
   Greek Colonies

Mediterranean Sea

● By 500BC the Greek world was large, rich and powerful. It stretched from France in the west to Turkey in the east.

● Wherever they went, the Greek settlers took their own way of life. They must have looked odd to the locals!

• The Greeks were a brilliant people. They had good laws and strong armies. They built beautiful temples and theatres. They were great thinkers, artists and athletes.

How did Greece grow bigger and bigger?

Greece and its homelands were small, with land that was rocky and hilly. By about 750BC, there was no room left for new towns or farms, and food began to run short. Because of this, many people left Greece to look for new places to live, and the Greek world began to grow.

Who was the goddess of wisdom?

The goddess Athene was the goddess of wisdom and war. Her symbol was the wise owl. But she also had special powers to protect the city of Athens. Because of this, the citizens loved and worshipped her. They built Athene her very own temple high above the city – the Parthenon.

● According to stories, the gods lived on top of Mount Olympus, the highest mountain in Greece. They spent a lot of their time quarrelling with one another.

Hermes messenger of the gods

Zeus king of the gods

Demeter goddess of plants

Aphrodite goddess of love and beauty

Hera queen of the gods, goddess of women and children

Hades god of the underworld

● The Greeks believed in many different gods and goddesses. Each one had different powers. Some of the gods were kind, but others were stern and cruel.

Who told stories about the gods?

A famous poet called Homer told many exciting stories about gods and heroes. His poem 'The Odyssey' tells the adventures of Odysseus, a Greek soldier sailing home to Ithaca. The sea god Poseidon tries to stop Odysseus getting home, but he's protected by the goddess Athene.

● Inside the Parthenon stood a towering statue of Athene – about ten times taller than you! It was made entirely of gold and ivory.

● Poseidon was god of the sea. He tried to sink Odysseus's ship by stirring up violent storms.

Who were the Romans?

The Romans were people who came from Rome. About 2,000 years ago they became so powerful that they began to conquer the lands around them. By AD100 they ruled a huge empire, and were one of the mightiest nations in the ancient world.

● An old legend says that the city of Rome was first started by a man called Romulus. He and his twin brother Remus had been abandoned by their parents and brought up by a wolf!

● Different parts of the empire had very different climates. Romans boiled in Egypt, where the summers were sweltering...

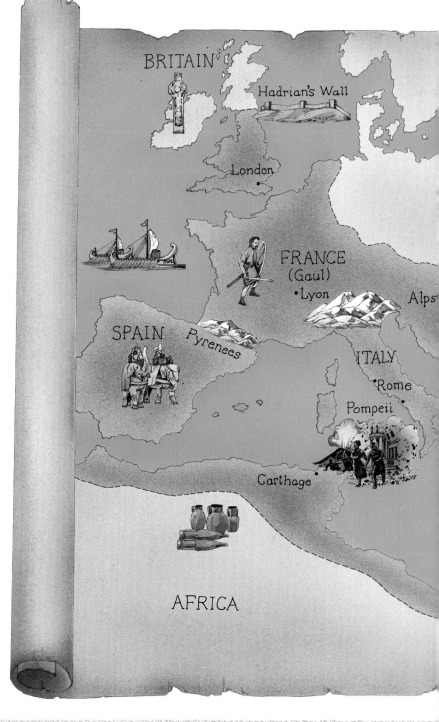

BRITAIN
Hadrian's Wall
London
FRANCE (Gaul)
•Lyon
Alps
SPAIN
Pyrenees
ITALY
•Rome
Pompeii
Carthage
AFRICA

Did all the Romans live in Rome?

● ...but they shivered in the icy mountains of Armenia. It was one of the coldest places in the whole empire.

The city of Rome wasn't big enough for all the Romans! All in all, there were about 50 million people in the empire, which stretched from Britain in the north to Africa in the south. Everyone in the empire was a Roman, and had to obey Roman laws.

THE ROMAN EMPIRE AD100

Caspian Sea

Black Sea

Constantinople

Athens Ephesus

ASIA MINOR

Antioch

SYRIA

Mediterranean Sea

ARABIA

N

Alexandria

EGYPT

Red Sea

● It would have taken nearly 100 days to ride from one end of the empire to the other. It was a journey of about 5,000 kilometres.

Where can you visit Ancient Rome?

Pompeii was a bustling town not far from Rome. In the year AD 79, a nearby volcano suddenly erupted, and buried the town in a layer of ash. The ash hardened, hiding Pompeii for hundreds of years. Then, one day, some Italian farmers discovered its Roman remains.

● Archaeologists have studied Pompeii since the 1800s, and have uncovered an almost-perfect Roman town.

MAKING MODELS

1 Dead people were buried by the ash. Over the years, their bodies rotted away, leaving people-shaped holes in the rock.

2 Archaeologists used the holes as moulds. They poured plaster inside, and waited for it to set.

3 Chipping away at the rock left plaster models of the Romans. Archaeologists study these carefully to learn about Roman life.

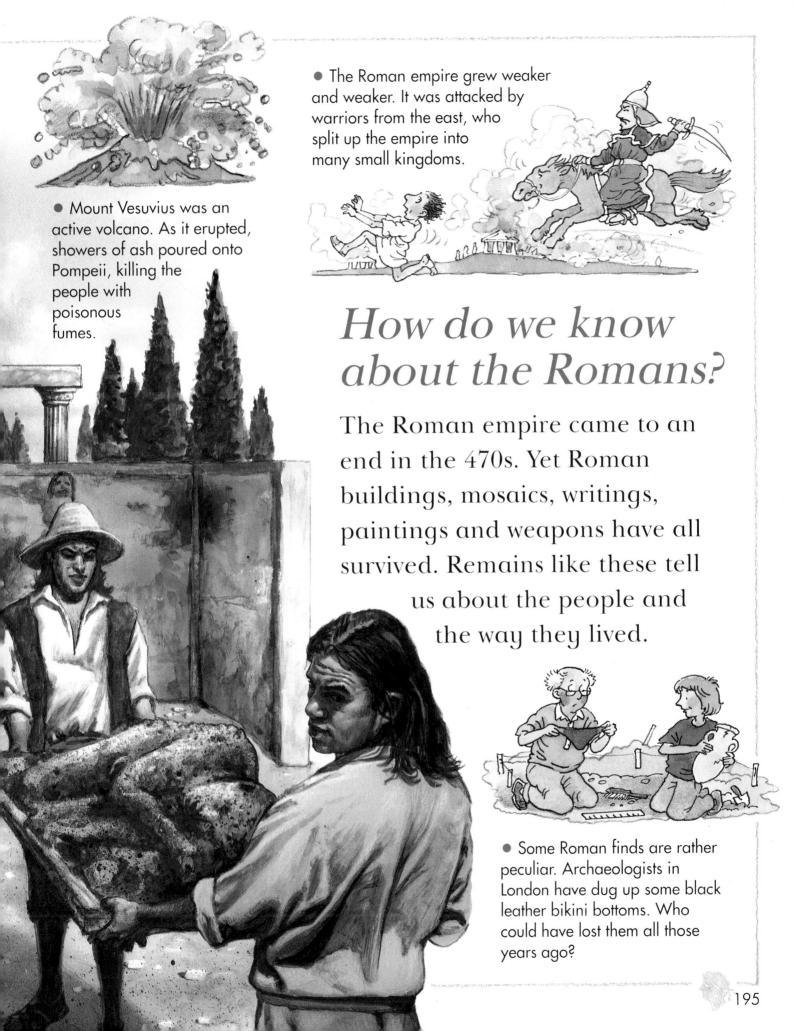

● Mount Vesuvius was an active volcano. As it erupted, showers of ash poured onto Pompeii, killing the people with poisonous fumes.

● The Roman empire grew weaker and weaker. It was attacked by warriors from the east, who split up the empire into many small kingdoms.

How do we know about the Romans?

The Roman empire came to an end in the 470s. Yet Roman buildings, mosaics, writings, paintings and weapons have all survived. Remains like these tell us about the people and the way they lived.

● Some Roman finds are rather peculiar. Archaeologists in London have dug up some black leather bikini bottoms. Who could have lost them all those years ago?

What were the Middle Ages in the middle of?

We call the years between the ancient world and the modern world in Europe the Middle Ages. They started in the 470s, when rule by the Romans came to an end, and they finished in the 1450s.

● The Romans once ruled most of Europe and North Africa. Then fierce warriors invaded, splitting Roman lands into many small kingdoms. By the 1450s Europe had larger countries again, more like those of today.

● In the Middle Ages, no one knew what the whole world looked like.

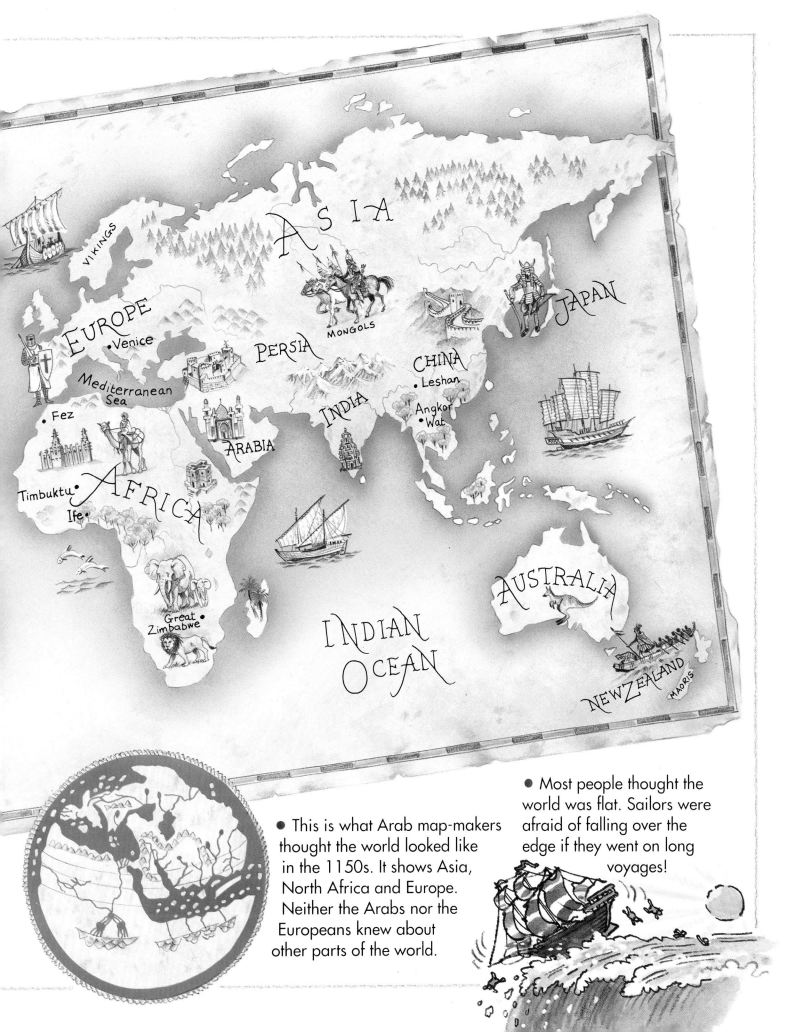

VIKINGS

ASIA

EUROPE

Venice

PERSIA

MONGOLS

JAPAN

CHINA

Leshan

Mediterranean Sea

Fez

INDIA

Angkor Wat

ARABIA

Timbuktu

AFRICA

Ife

Great Zimbabwe

INDIAN OCEAN

AUSTRALIA

NEW ZEALAND

MAORIS

● This is what Arab map-makers thought the world looked like in the 1150s. It shows Asia, North Africa and Europe. Neither the Arabs nor the Europeans knew about other parts of the world.

● Most people thought the world was flat. Sailors were afraid of falling over the edge if they went on long voyages!

Why did castles have moats?

Moats were deep wide ditches filled with water, which made it harder for enemies to break into a castle. Friendly visitors could cross the moat over a drawbridge. But when enemies attacked, the drawbridge was raised.

● Spies and traitors were chained up in the castle's dungeons. These were dark and damp and full of rats and spiders!

● One way to beat enemies who shut themselves up in a castle was to surround it – and wait! This was called a siege. When the castle ran out of food and water, the people inside had to give in.

● Strong stone walls were built to protect towns and cities all over the world. The picture on the right shows Great Zimbabwe, a walled city begun in the 1000s by the Shona people of southern Africa.

● Pueblo Bonito was one of the walled towns built by the Anasazi people of North America between 950 and 1300.

● In the 1300s, people in Europe learned how to make big guns called cannons. In time it became easier to blow up castles – if the guns went off properly!

Why did knights wear armour?

In battle, knights were bashed and battered about by swords, arrows, axes, long pointed lances and metal clubs called maces. They had to protect their bodies from all these sharp weapons, so they wore suits of tough metal armour.

- Until the 1200s most knights wore chain-mail armour. This was made from linked metal rings. Later armour was made from solid metal plates.

  By the end of the Middle Ages, a knight was like a can of beans on legs – completely covered in metal!

- Putting on armour wasn't easy. A squire was a boy who was learning to be a knight. He helped the knight get ready for battle.

  Armour wasn't very comfortable to wear, so knights put on thick padded clothes underneath.

● Japanese knights were called samurai. Their armour was made of metal plates fixed to padded silk and leather.

● Bows and deadly arrows were used by soldiers in most parts of the world.

Welsh longbowman

Turkish crossbowman

Aztec warrior

Mongol archer

● A samurai always had a bath before going into battle. Then, if he died, he knew he would be clean and ready to go to heaven.

Where was Vinland the Good?

Viking sailors from Scandinavia were the first Europeans to cross the Atlantic Ocean and reach North America. They landed on the east coast in the early 1000s and named it Vinland, or Vineland, because they found lots of grapevines there.

● No one is quite certain where Vinland was, but the most likely place is Newfoundland, in what is Canada today. People now think the Vikings found cranberries or gooseberries there, not grapes!

Who went to sea in junks?

By the 1400s, Chinese junks were the world's biggest ships. The largest were five times the size of ships being built in Europe.

Junk

European ship

- A Moroccan called Ibn Batuta spent 30 years travelling. He went east to India, China and Sumatra, and south to Timbuktu, in Africa. He lived in the 1300s.

- One of the great explorers of the Middle Ages was a Venetian called Marco Polo. It took him four whole years to travel to China.

- Polynesian sailors explored the vast South Pacific Ocean in nothing bigger than canoes. The Maoris are descended from Polynesians who reached New Zealand about 1,000 years ago.

Was Sinbad a real sailor?

The exciting adventures of Sinbad the Sailor were folktales made up by Persian storytellers in the Middle Ages. Although Sinbad was make-believe, there were lots of real people making amazing journeys over land and across the ocean.

Where did Robin Hood live?

The stories about Robin Hood say he lived in Sherwood Forest, near the English town of Nottingham. He and his Merry Men were outlaws, because they broke the law by robbing the rich, but they gave the money to poor people.

● Was there really such a person as Robin Hood? Nobody knows for sure. Some people think he was an outlaw called Robert Fitzooth, the Earl of Huntingdon.

● People have told stories about Robin Hood, Maid Marian and the Merry Men since the 1300s.

● Everyone enjoys a good story. Today we can look at books or watch films and videos. In the Middle Ages, people loved to listen to storytellers.

Who was Joan of Arc?

Joan was a French peasant girl who grew up at a time when England and France were at war. In 1429, at the age of 17, she dressed up as a soldier and helped to free the city of Orleans from an English army. But just a year later she was captured and burnt at the stake.

Who was a teenage warrior?

Temujin was the son of a leader of the Mongol people of central Asia. He was born in 1162 and he became a warrior when he was only 13, after his father died. He took the name Genghis Khan. Under his leadership, the Mongols attacked and won many lands in Asia.

Who were the Tudors?

The Tudors were kings and queens who ruled England for nearly 200 years. They were called the Tudors because Tudor was their surname. The most famous of them was Henry VIII, who ruled during the 1500s.

- The *Mary Rose* was the pride and joy of Henry's navy. A fortune was spent on doing it up, but when the royals went to see it set out it sank before it even left the port!

- The rich wore clothes of velvet and lace, with pearls or other precious jewels sewn on. They looked beautiful, but they smelt terrible – they hardly ever had a bath!

UNDER NEW OWNERSHIP

- Henry VIII was the first head of the Church of England. He closed down the Catholic monasteries and spent the riches on his wars, or on building new manor houses.

• The Spanish sent a fleet of ships to invade England in 1558. Francis Drake, the head of the English navy, had no worries that the Spanish would win. He even finished the game of bowls he was playing before he went to fight them!

What happened to the Aztecs?

The Aztecs were a rich and powerful people who lived in South America. But they were defeated by Cortés in 1521. He ransacked their cities for gold and other riches, which he took back to the Queen in Spain.

• Queen Elizabeth I was the last of the Tudors. She never married so when she died, her distant cousin, James VI of Scotland, became king of England too. His surname was Stuart, so the next lot of rulers were called the Stuarts.

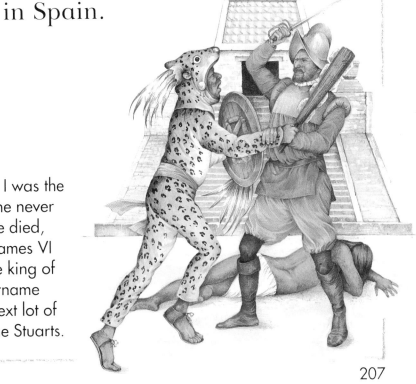

Who made a new home in the New World?

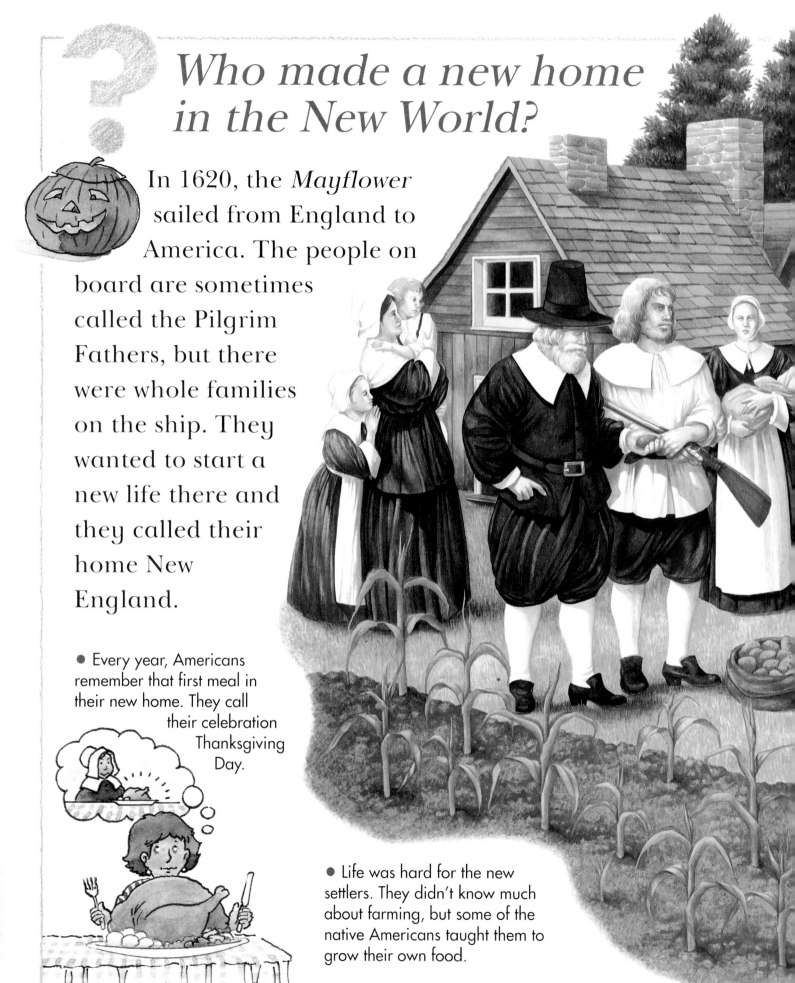

In 1620, the *Mayflower* sailed from England to America. The people on board are sometimes called the Pilgrim Fathers, but there were whole families on the ship. They wanted to start a new life there and they called their home New England.

● Every year, Americans remember that first meal in their new home. They call their celebration Thanksgiving Day.

● Life was hard for the new settlers. They didn't know much about farming, but some of the native Americans taught them to grow their own food.

- The Pilgrim Fathers left England because they weren't happy with the king. They weren't the only ones! In 1605 there'd been a plot to blow him up when he opened Parliament – the Gunpowder Plot.

Who built the best home for the next world?

The Taj Mahal is a magnificent tomb in India. The Mogul ruler, Shah Jahan built it for his favourite wife, who died in 1629. It was made of white marble and took 21 years to build. The outside is decorated with flowers and passages from the Muslim holy book, *The Koran*.

- The explorer Christopher Columbus discovered America in 1492. No one had ever sailed so far west. Some people thought he might fall off the edge of the world!

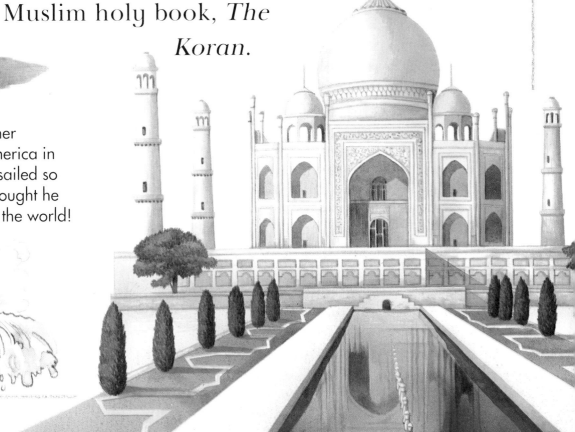

Who was the 'last' king of France?

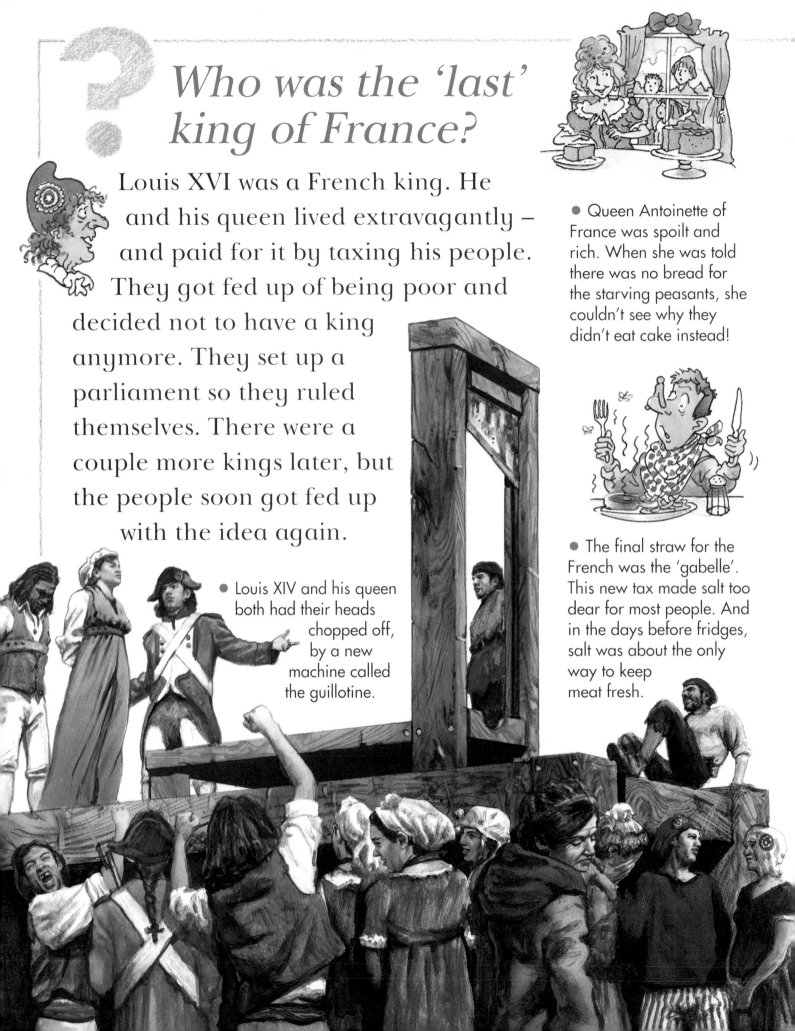

Louis XVI was a French king. He and his queen lived extravagantly – and paid for it by taxing his people. They got fed up of being poor and decided not to have a king anymore. They set up a parliament so they ruled themselves. There were a couple more kings later, but the people soon got fed up with the idea again.

● Queen Antoinette of France was spoilt and rich. When she was told there was no bread for the starving peasants, she couldn't see why they didn't eat cake instead!

● Louis XIV and his queen both had their heads chopped off, by a new machine called the guillotine.

● The final straw for the French was the 'gabelle'. This new tax made salt too dear for most people. And in the days before fridges, salt was about the only way to keep meat fresh.

● President Washington's head can still be seen on coins and bank-notes today.

● The United States had to fight to become free, or independent of Britain. The war was called the War of Independence.

Who was the first president of the United States?

George Washington became the first United States president in 1789. Before then, the British king had ruled the United States – from nearly 5,000 kilometres across the the ocean.

● The American people were fed up with paying taxes to the British king. One night a few of them ransacked a British tea ship in Boston harbour and threw all the tea chests overboard. We call it the Boston Tea Party – some party!

Who steamed into the twentieth century?

Many of today's machines were invented in the 1800s. Factories were built and people grew richer. It was cheaper and quicker to make things, such as clothes. Nowadays we call this time the industrial revolution, because there were so many changes in industry.

● Inventions like the new steam trains changed everyone's lives. It meant more people could afford to travel.

● The Great Exhibition of 1851 was to show off all the new goods that were being made. Even the building was amazing – the Crystal Palace was built entirely of glass and steel.

● All this industry needed power, which came from coal. Even children worked in the coal mines – because they were small they could get into the tiniest tunnels.

● Families were a lot bigger in the 1800s than they are today. Many families had ten children or even more!

COUNTRIES
AND
PEOPLES

What is a country?

A country is an independent land with its own government. The government runs the country, and makes laws which the people must keep. A country has its own name, and its borders are normally agreed by other countries around the world.

● Each country has its own money, called its currency, with its own style of coins and bank-notes. There are roubles in Russia and francs in France.

● All countries have their own stamps, which often carry a picture of the country's ruler. Some stamps show a country's wildlife, or mark an important discovery.

● People wave their national flags at parades, sports events and celebrations.

CHINA

BRAZIL

SWEDEN

GREECE

GERMANY

ISRAEL

Why do countries fly flags?

Every country has its own flag, which is a sort of national badge. Each flag is different. Its design may include coloured stripes, star and sun patterns, or religious signs such as crosses or crescents. Flags are flown on special occasions, as a symbol of a country and its people.

● Every country has its own special song called a national anthem. It is sung to show respect for a country and its history.

SUDAN

AUSTRALIA

UNITED KINGDOM

CANADA

TURKEY

ARGENTINA

SOUTH KOREA

JAMAICA

AUSTRIA

How many countries are there?

There are about 190 independent countries in the world, but the number changes from year to year. This is because new countries are sometimes made, or two countries may join together, as East and West Germany did in 1990.

1 Guatemala
2 Belize
3 El Salvador
4 Honduras
5 Nicaragua
6 Costa Rica
7 Panama
8 Cuba
9 Bahamas
10 Jamaica
11 Haiti
12 Dominican Republic
13 Antigua & Barbuda
14 Dominica
15 Barbados
16 St Vincent & Grenadines
17 Trinidad & Tobago
18 Ecuador
19 Ireland
20 United Kingdom
21 Belgium
22 Netherlands
23 Luxembourg

24 Switzerland
25 Liechtenstein
26 San Marino
27 Vatican City
28 Italy
29 Monaco
30 Andorra
31 Denmark
32 Estonia
33 Latvia
34 Lithuania
35 Czech Republic
36 Austria
37 Slovakia
38 Hungary
39 Slovenia
40 Croatia
41 Bosnia & Herzogovina
42 Yugoslavia
43 Macedonia
44 Albania
45 Greece
46 Bulgaria
47 Moldova

48 Malta
49 Cyprus
50 Lebanon
51 Israel
52 Jordan
53 Armenia
54 Azerbaijan
55 Kuwait
56 Bahrain
57 Qatar
58 United Arab Emirates

- Some small Pacific island countries are not shown on this map: Fiji, Kiribati, Marshall Islands, Federated States of Micronesia, Nauru, Palau, Tonga, Tuvalu and Western Samoa.

59 Tajikistan
60 Kyrgyzstan
61 Bhutan
62 Bangladesh
63 Sri Lanka

64 Singapore
65 Brunei
66 Eritrea
67 Djibouti
68 Uganda
69 Rwanda
70 Burundi
71 Malawi
72 Zimbabwe
73 Swaziland
74 Lesotho
75 Equatorial Guinea
76 Togo

77 Liberia
78 Sierra Leone
79 Guinea
80 Guinea-Bissau
81 Gambia
82 Senegal
83 Burkina Faso
84 Tunisia

Which country has the most people?

Well over a billion people live in China, and about 48,000 new babies are born there every day. You'd think that meant a lot of birthdays, but in China everyone celebrates their birthday at the same time – the Chinese New Year!

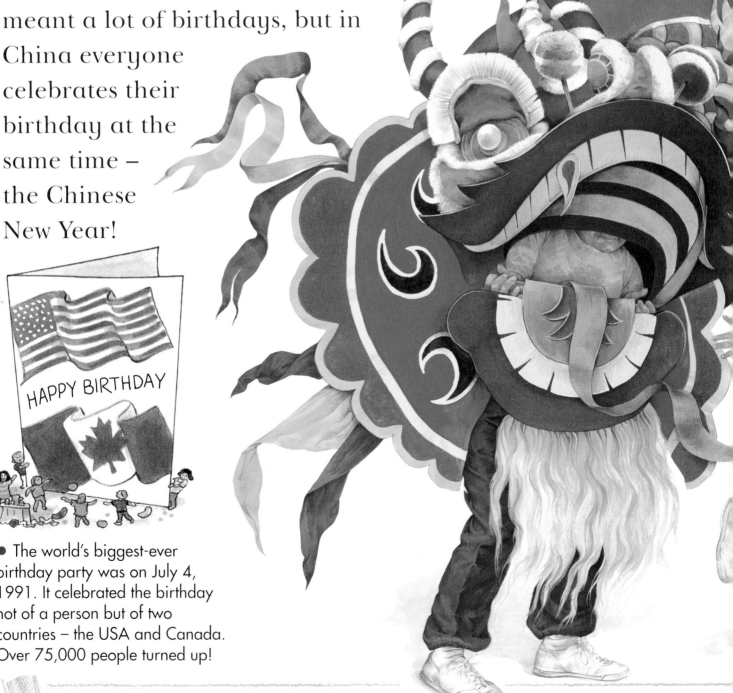

● Chinese New Year is celebrated by Chinese people all over the world in late January or early February. There are spectacular street processions.

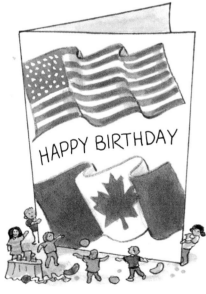

HAPPY BIRTHDAY

● The world's biggest-ever birthday party was on July 4, 1991. It celebrated the birthday not of a person but of two countries – the USA and Canada. Over 75,000 people turned up!

Which is the biggest country?

Russia is so big that it takes eight days to cross it by train! As children set off for school in the city of Moscow in the west, others are already going home in the eastern port of Vladivostok.

MOSCOW

VLADIVOSTOK

Where is there land, but no countries?

The vast frozen land around the South Pole is called Antarctica. It is not a country – it has no people, no government and no flag. Many countries have signed an agreement, promising to keep Antarctica as a wilderness for scientists to study.

● Nobody lives in Antarctica except for a few hundred scientists, who go there to study rocks, the weather, and the plant and animal life.

Where are there only two seasons?

Many tropical countries have only two seasons in the year. One is very wet, and the other very dry. Not many trees manage to survive the dry months, and animals travel hundreds of kilometres searching for food and water.

● Many animals migrate in different seasons. Every year, swarms of monarch butterflies leave Mexico and fly 3,000 kilometres to spend the summer by cool Canadian lakes.

● During the dry season, the ground is baked hard by the hot Sun. Clouds of dust cover everything and everyone.

● In the dry season, herds of wildebeest and zebra cross the grasslands of central Africa. They follow the thunderclouds in search of rainwater and fresh grass.

EQUATOR

● Tropical lands lie near the equator. They are the warmest parts of the Earth.

Where does it pour for a month?

Some parts of India and Southeast Asia have long heavy downpours called monsoons. Big black clouds are blown in from the sea during the summer months. Once the rain starts, it can last for weeks, flooding the fields and the streets.

Which city is above the clouds?

The city of Lhasa is in Tibet, a part of China. It is built near the edge of the Himalayas, the world's highest mountains. Lhasa is so high that it's often covered by clouds, which blanket the city in a thick wet mist!

● Some people call Tibet the Roof of the World, because it so high up in the mountains.

Why do Venetians walk on water?

The Italian city of Venice is built on dozens of tiny islands in a sheltered lagoon near the sea. In between the islands are canals, which form the main 'streets' of the city. To get from one part of Venice to another, you don't take a bus or a train – you catch a motor boat or a gondola.

● A country's capital city is where the government works. Washington DC is the capital of the USA. The President lives there, in the White House.

● You have to climb 1,000 steps to reach the Potala Palace, which towers above the streets of Lhasa. It's very grand – even its roofs are made of gold!

Which is the world's biggest city?

Over 21 million people live in Mexico's capital. Mexico City is already home to more people than live in the whole of Australia, and it's growing fast!

Who rides on a snowmobile?

Many of the people who live in icy Alaska and northern Canada travel across the frozen snow on powerful sleds called snowmobiles. Not long ago, sleds were pulled by husky dogs, but nowadays these are only raced for fun.

● A dog team can pull a sled about 80 kilometres in a day. A snowmobile covers that in an hour!

● Trains in Tokyo, Japan, are so crowded that railway staff called crushers have to push in the passengers while the doors close.

● Fishermen in Portugal paint 'magic' eyes on their boats to watch over them at sea and bring them safely to harbour.

Where do you park your bike in China?

There are millions and millions of people in China, and millions and millions of bikes! So all Chinese cities have huge cycle parks, where an attendant gives your bike a number, and helps you to find it again later.

Who paints pictures on trucks?

The truck drivers of Afghanistan are very proud of their trucks. They paint holy pictures all over them, covering every last centimetre in bright, colourful patterns. Even the wheel nuts are painted different colours.

● The Afghans may drape their trucks with silver chains, and even stick on ring-pulls from drink cans as decorations.

Who writes with a paintbrush?

In China and Japan, handwriting can be an art. Instead of dashing something off with a pen, people sometimes paint words slowly and beautifully with a brush and ink. Artists often frame their work, and hang it on the wall just like a picture.

● About 50,000 different symbols may be used to write Chinese. Luckily, school children only have to learn about 5,000 of them.

● The art of beautiful handwriting is called calligraphy. Japanese children learn calligraphy at school.

Who reads back-to-front?

To read a book in Arabic or Hebrew, you have to work from right to left. So if this book were in Arabic, the first page would be where the index is now.

Which country speaks over 800 languages?

Papua New Guinea is a land of many languages. Most of the people live in small villages, deep in the rainforest or high up in the misty mountains. Some are so cut off from each other that their languages are quite different.

● In many areas of Papua New Guinea, people can only talk to each other through a translator.

● Around 5,000 languages are spoken around the world. Here are just a few ways to say "hello".

Jambo! Namaste! ¡Hola! Czesc! Dag!

Swahili Hindi Spanish Polish Dutch

● There's a place in New Zealand with 85 letters in its name. And there's another in France with just one!

Taumatawhakatangihangakoauauotamateaturipukakapikimaungahoronukupokaiwhenuakitanatahu

Which is the oldest dish on the menu?

● All over the world, people pound grains such as maize to make flour for their pancakes.

Pancakes may be the oldest dish of all. Even Stone Age people baked them! The basic recipe – milk, eggs and flour – is the same the world over, but the kind of flour changes from place to place. Pancakes can be made using flour from potatoes, maize, wheat or oats.

● In different parts of the world you might find almost anything on your plate – from crunchy insects or chewy snails, to snakes, guinea pigs, or even sheep's eyes!

Who eats shells, butterflies and little worms?

We do! These are all types of pasta – their Italian names are conchiglie (shells), farfalle (butterflies) and vermicelli (little worms). Pasta is a dough made from flour and water, which is cut into shapes and cooked. It's simply delicious served with a tasty sauce and a sprinkling of cheese.

Vermicelli

Farfalle

Conchiglie

● Table manners change from place to place. The British think you're rude if you put your elbows on the table, while the French think it's perfectly all right!

● Pasta dough comes in over 100 shapes and sizes. It's cut into stars, shells, snail shapes, and all the letters of the alphabet.

Where does it take all afternoon to have a cup of tea?

In Japan there's a special ancient tea ceremony called chanoyu. The tea is made so slowly, and sipped so carefully, that it really does take hours. It's not a good idea to turn up to the ceremony feeling thirsty!

Where are wheatfields bigger than countries?

The rolling grasslands of Canada and the USA are planted with wheat as far as the eye can see. One Canadian wheatfield was so big, it was double the size of the European country, San Marino!

● Huge combine harvesters have to work in teams to harvest the gigantic wheatfields.

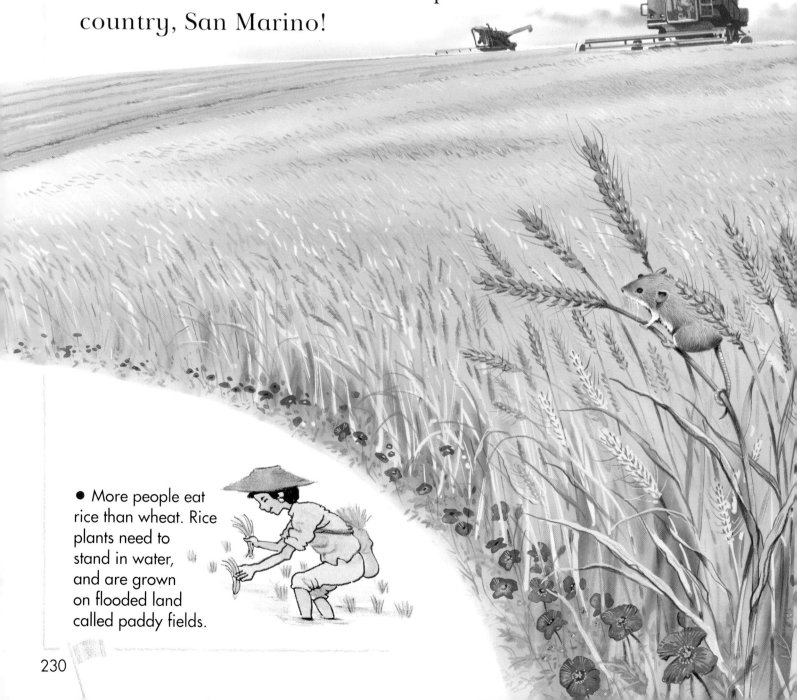

● More people eat rice than wheat. Rice plants need to stand in water, and are grown on flooded land called paddy fields.

Where does chocolate grow on trees?

Chocolate is made from the seeds of the cacao tree. Sadly, the trees don't grow everywhere – just in the hot, wet parts of South America, southeast Asia and West Africa.

Which country has more sheep than people?

● In Thailand, coconut farmers train monkeys to harvest their crop. The monkeys scamper up the trunks of the palm trees and throw down the fruits.

Although there are more than 17 million people in Australia, most live around the coast. In the centre people run enormous sheep farms. At the last count, there were 147 million sheep – nearly nine times the number of people!

Where do women wear bowler hats?

In the Andes Mountains of South America, many of the women wear round bowler hats. The hat has become a part of their traditional dress, along with full skirts and brilliantly-coloured llama-wool shawls and ponchos.

● Lake Titicaca, up in the Andes, is the highest lake in the world. The people there use reed boats to travel between islands.

● Bowler hats were first made for men, not women! British businessmen have worn them to work for over 100 years.

Where do men wear skirts?

On special occasions in the Highlands of Scotland, it's traditional for men to wear kilts. These pleated skirts are made of a checked woollen cloth called tartan. Kilts are warm, but they only come down to the knee, so they are worn with a pair of long, woolly socks.

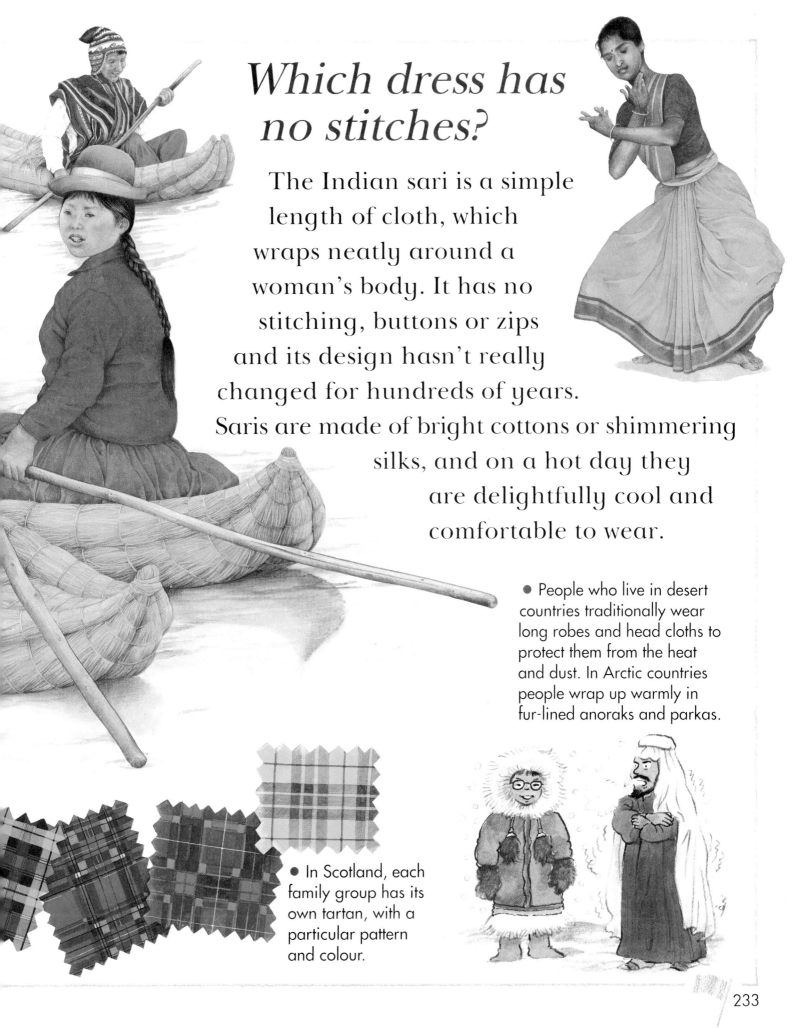

Which dress has no stitches?

The Indian sari is a simple length of cloth, which wraps neatly around a woman's body. It has no stitching, buttons or zips and its design hasn't really changed for hundreds of years. Saris are made of bright cottons or shimmering silks, and on a hot day they are delightfully cool and comfortable to wear.

● People who live in desert countries traditionally wear long robes and head cloths to protect them from the heat and dust. In Arctic countries people wrap up warmly in fur-lined anoraks and parkas.

● In Scotland, each family group has its own tartan, with a particular pattern and colour.

Who wears bank-notes at their wedding?

At a Greek or Turkish wedding, the guests don't take the bride and groom gifts – they give them money instead. At the wedding party, guests pin bank-notes all over the couple's clothes. Often there is so much money that it completely covers their clothes!

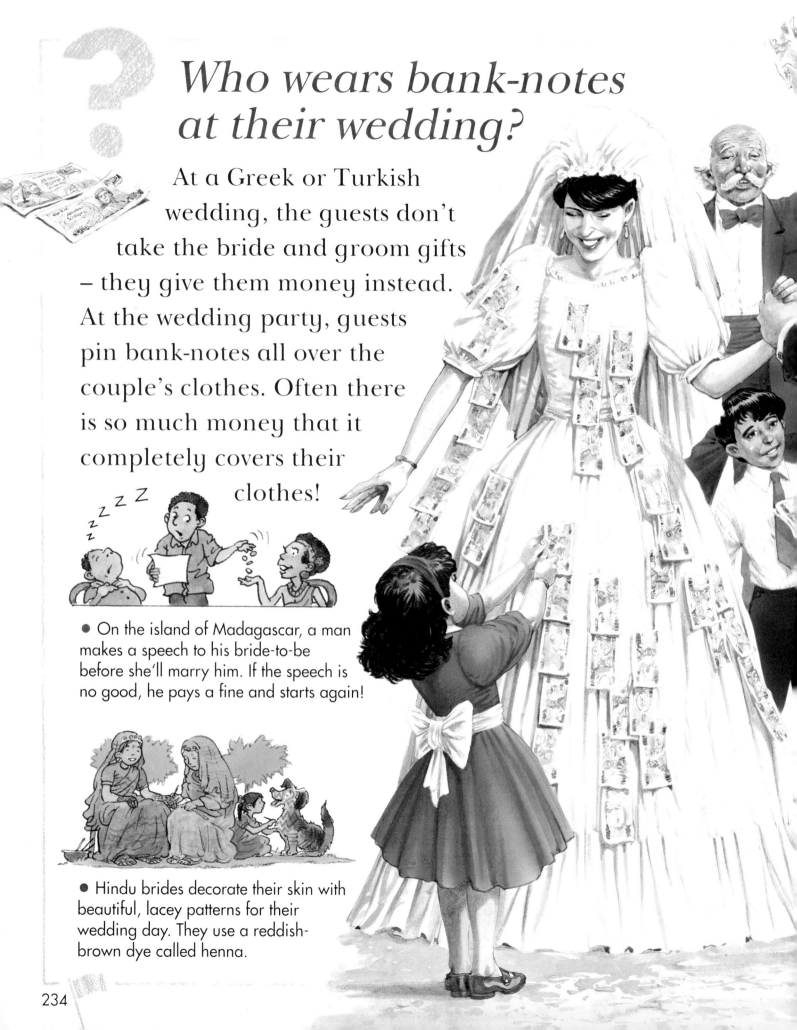

● On the island of Madagascar, a man makes a speech to his bride-to-be before she'll marry him. If the speech is no good, he pays a fine and starts again!

● Hindu brides decorate their skin with beautiful, lacey patterns for their wedding day. They use a reddish-brown dye called henna.

Where are children made kings and queens?

On January 6th, French families enjoy a special dinner together. At the end of the meal, the children eat slices of a flat almond pie called a galette. In one of the slices a charm is hidden, and whoever finds it is crowned king or queen for the night.

• Three kings from the East are said to have visited the two-week-old baby Jesus on January 6th.

Who sticks out their tongue at strangers?

One of the customs of the Maori people of New Zealand is to stick out their tongues, pull faces and make loud noises, to scare strangers who come to their village, or marae, before accepting them as friends.

Who lights the lamps at New Year?

The Hindu New Year is called the Festival of Light – and no wonder! Towns are strung with lights, and lamps shine from every door and window. The women make beautiful floor pictures with coloured chalks, flour and sand, and decorate them with glowing candles.

● Chinese New Year celebrations can last up to 15 days. They begin between the middle of January and the middle of February.

Who brings in the New Year with a bang?

New Year in China starts with beating drums, crashing cymbals, fireworks and a lion or dragon dancing through the streets. All this noise is meant to chase away the bad days of the past and bring luck in the future.

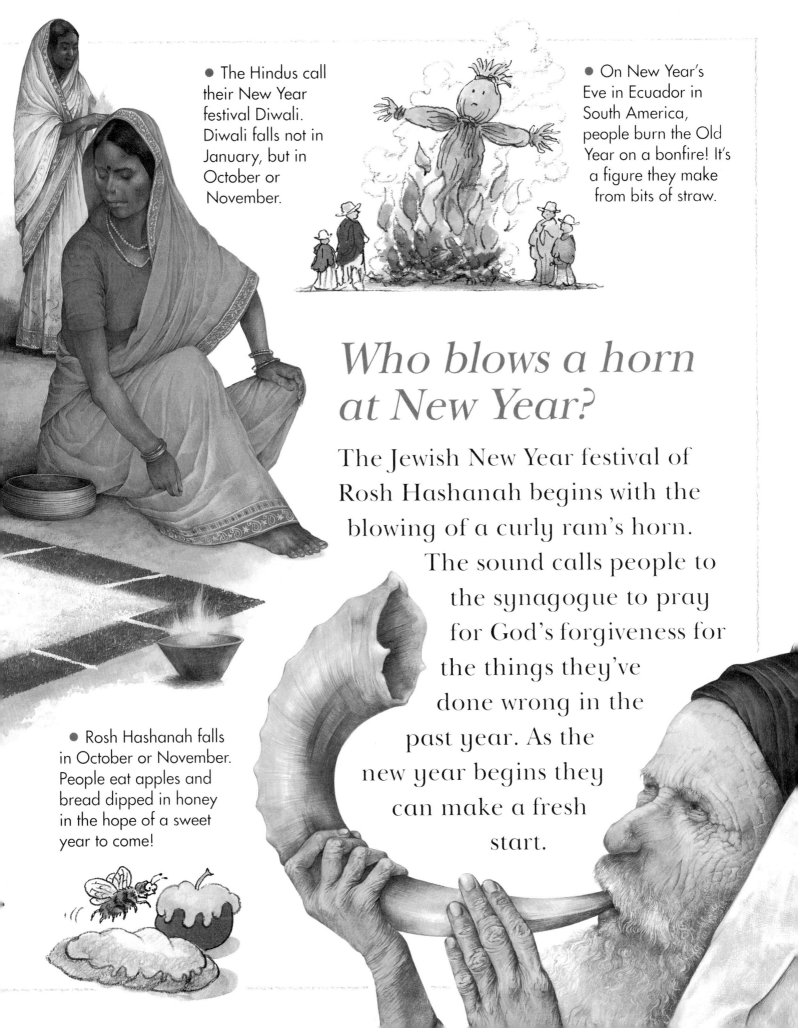

● The Hindus call their New Year festival Diwali. Diwali falls not in January, but in October or November.

● On New Year's Eve in Ecuador in South America, people burn the Old Year on a bonfire! It's a figure they make from bits of straw.

Who blows a horn at New Year?

The Jewish New Year festival of Rosh Hashanah begins with the blowing of a curly ram's horn. The sound calls people to the synagogue to pray for God's forgiveness for the things they've done wrong in the past year. As the new year begins they can make a fresh start.

● Rosh Hashanah falls in October or November. People eat apples and bread dipped in honey in the hope of a sweet year to come!

Where do elephants glow in the dark?

For the Sri Lankan festival of the Esala Perahera, elephants are decorated with beautiful hangings and strings of electric lights. More than 50 elephants take part in a night-time procession, along with thousands of drummers and dancers, who crack whips and wave colourful banners.

● The leprechaun of Irish folktales is a little green man. The green shamrock is Ireland's national flower.

When do people eat green food?

Saint Patrick is the patron saint of Ireland, and green is the country's national colour. Saint Patrick's Day falls on March 17th, and for Irish people everywhere it's a time of wild celebration. Some people even dye party food and drink green!

When is the Day of the Dead?

The Day of the Dead is a Mexican holiday which takes place every year on November 2nd, All Soul's Day. People remember dead friends and relatives by taking flowers and candles to their graves, and having picnics there.

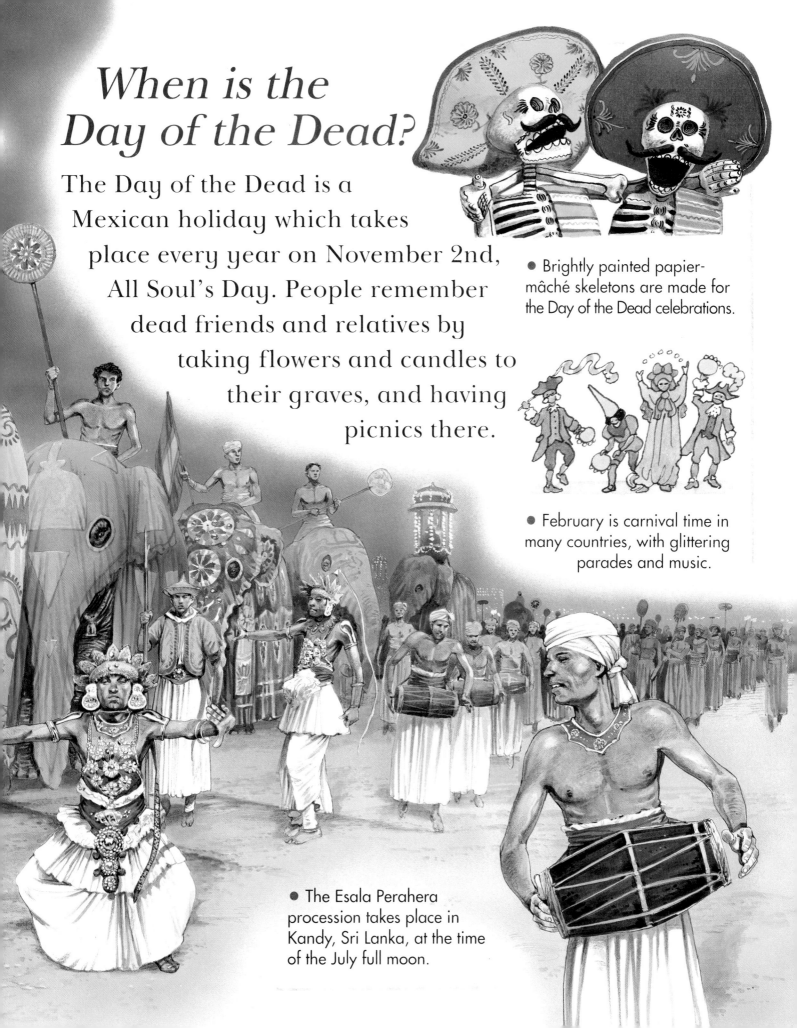

● Brightly painted papier-mâché skeletons are made for the Day of the Dead celebrations.

● February is carnival time in many countries, with glittering parades and music.

● The Esala Perahera procession takes place in Kandy, Sri Lanka, at the time of the July full moon.

Where can you play an oil drum?

In the Caribbean islands, large empty oil drums are made into musical drums called steel pans. The top is hammered into a curved dish-shape. Then this metal dish is beaten and 'tuned' until the different parts of the steel pan make a number of musical sounds. Some drums can play 30 different notes.

● Steel bands play outside in the streets or on the beach at carnival time.

Who bangs on the bongos?

A drummer in a South American dance band often plays the bongos. He grips the drums between his knees and taps them with his fingers and the palm of his hand. This makes zippy rhythms that soon get you dancing.

Can drums talk?

In Nigeria, talking drums can even tell the news. The kalangu drum's beats are like a secret language that only a few people are able to understand. The drummer tightens or loosens the drum skin to change the sounds.

● The Tinguian people of the Philippines thought that the sound of thunder was the god Kadaklan, pounding on his drum.

● A lion-roar drum sounds rather like a real lion – scary! You don't beat this drum. Instead you pull a stick or strip of leather through a hole in the top, and a growling noise rumbles out.

Where can you find a gamelan?

A gamelan is a kind of orchestra from Indonesia. Drums, gongs, xylophones and chimes all play together to make a magical tinkling sound. There can be as many as 40 instruments in a gamelan.

● Washboards are just trays to scrub clothes on. But some jazz musicians play them like an instrument. They scrape a stick or thimble across the ridges.

● Gamelan players treat their instruments with great respect.

Are rattles just for babies?

It isn't only babies who like the dry, swishing sound rattles make. The first ones were probably dried plant pods, full of seeds. South American rattles called maracas are still often filled with dried beans. You could fill a yoghurt pot with some to make your own rattle.

● The triangle is one of the smallest instruments. Larger triangles are used to warn people about fire in some parts of the world, but sirens work better on noisy roads!

What roars like a bull?

The bull-roarer doesn't really roar like an angry bull! It's a block of wood fixed to a piece of string. You whirl it above your head and it makes a strange screaming noise.

243

How do termites help to make music?

The didgeridoo is a long, musical pipe from Australia. It's made from a log of the eucalyptus tree, which is buried inside a termites' mound. The wood-eating termites gnaw away at the soft wood inside the log, leaving a hollow pipe. Then the pipe is decorated. These days, some didgeridoos are hollowed out by hand, but they don't give the same rich sound.

Which harp fits inside your mouth?

The tiny Jew's harp doesn't look like a proper harp. You put it between your teeth, and twang its metal tongue with your finger. It makes your lips feel funny because the metal vibrates so much.

● Didgeridoo-players can breathe in at the same time as they're blowing out through their instrument.

● The Masai people of Kenya play an instrument called a thumb piano. It has metal strips which you pluck with your thumb.

Which instrument is made with a spider's web?

If you take a cow's horn, make a little hole at the pointed end, and cover the wide end with a tough kind of spider's web, you've got a mirliton. Mirlitons are played in Africa. They make a buzzy sound when you blow or sing through them.

● An American jazz musician called Roland Kirk could play three saxophones all at once! He must have had lots of puff!

● Not all bagpipes come from Scotland. This Hungarian goatskin bagpipe has been decorated with a carved wooden goat's head!

Where do children watch shadows?

Shadow puppet shows are enjoyed by people all over the world. On the Indonesian island of Java, the audience sits on both sides of a cloth screen. One side watches the puppets while the other sees the shadows dance, as if by magic!

● Javanese puppets are made of painted leather. The puppeteer moves them with wires or rods.

● In a Vietnamese water puppet show, the story is acted out on the surface of a lake. It can't be much fun for the puppeteers – they have to stand in the water.

Who makes pictures from sand?

The Navajo people of the southwestern United States create beautiful pictures with grains of coloured sand. The pictures are made on the ground for special ceremonies. But these works of art don't last long – they are destroyed afterwards!

• Some sand pictures are said to have healing powers and are large enough for someone ill to sit in the middle of them.

• In Switzerland, cow herders used to play alpenhorns – long wooden horns which echoed from one mountain to another.

Which dancers snap their fingers?

Flamenco dancing comes from southern Spain. Proud-looking dancers toss their heads and snap their fingers, as they stamp and whirl to the music of a Spanish guitar.

Why do people race camels?

One-humped camels are so sturdy and fast that in hot desert areas they are ridden like racehorses. The races are very popular in Saudi Arabia, and large crowds cheer the camels as they speed across desert racetracks.

● Dromedaries can race at over 20 kilometres an hour – faster than two-humped camels.

● People have been known to race all sorts and sizes of animal – from ostriches to snails!

● The world's fastest ball game is called pelota. The ball is hurled from a wicker scoop at the speed of an express train.

Which is the world's most popular sport?

Footballs are kicked about in more than 160 countries around the world. The game is played by thousands of people, in playgrounds, parks, streets and, of course, football grounds.

● The earliest football-like game was called zuqiu. It was played 2,400 years ago in Ancient China.

Who lives in a longhouse?

On the tropical island of Borneo, some people live in long, airy buildings, which are made of wood and bamboo, and are raised on stilts. These longhouses are home to dozens of different families, each with their own room.

● As many as 100 families may share the same longhouse.

● Tower blocks are another way of squeezing a lot of homes into a small space. You find them in big towns and cities.

Where do gardens grow on rivers?

In the Netherlands, many people live on barges moored on the country's canals. Boat-owners don't have gardens, of course, but some of them grow flowers on the roof!

How do you keep cosy in the Gobi?

The Gobi Desert is in Mongolia in northern Asia and its winters are icy cold. Some shepherds and their families travel around the desert, living in thick, felt tents called yurts, which keep out the hot sun or the freezing cold.

Could people live in space?

They already have! Some astronauts have lived in space stations spinning around the Earth for as long as a year. There are plans for much bigger stations, where people could live for 10 years, and even for settlements on Mars.

● It would take 8 months to reach Mars in a spacecraft. The crew would have to take everything they needed with them – the food for just one person would make a pile twice as big as a family car.

● There are plans for a huge wheel-shaped space station, measuring over 1 kilometre across.

● People have even lived under the sea, but not for longer than a few weeks at a time. They were working in underwater laboratories.

ANIMALS
VOLUME I

- Female Queen Alexandra's birdwings are the world's biggest butterflies. Their wings are almost as big as this page!

- The blue whale is so long that eight elephants could stand along its back.

Giraffe
5.5 metres tall

Elephant
3.5 metres tall
7 tonnes

Ostrich
2.5 metres tall

- The giraffe is the tallest land animal. With its long neck, it can reach as high as a two-storey house.

- The mighty African elephant is almost three times as tall as you are. It can weigh as much as seven cars.

- The ostrich is the world's tallest and heaviest bird. It's as tall as a single-decker bus!

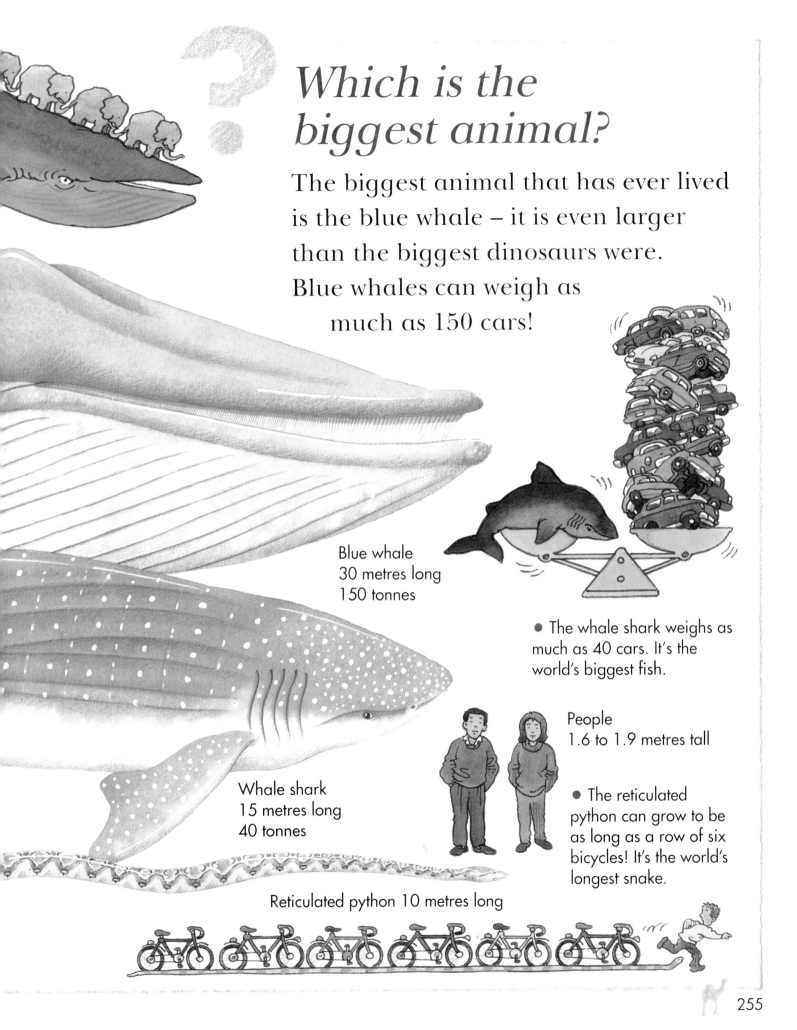

Which is the biggest animal?

The biggest animal that has ever lived is the blue whale – it is even larger than the biggest dinosaurs were. Blue whales can weigh as much as 150 cars!

Blue whale
30 metres long
150 tonnes

● The whale shark weighs as much as 40 cars. It's the world's biggest fish.

People
1.6 to 1.9 metres tall

Whale shark
15 metres long
40 tonnes

● The reticulated python can grow to be as long as a row of six bicycles! It's the world's longest snake.

Reticulated python 10 metres long

What's the difference between sharks and dolphins?

Although sharks and dolphins look alike, they belong to two very different animal groups. Sharks are a kind of fish, but dolphins are members of another group, the mammals.

- You don't look anything like a dolphin, but you are a mammal, too!

- If an animal breathes air through lungs, and its babies feed on their mother's milk, it's a mammal. Most mammals have some fur or hair on their bodies.

Lungs

● If an animal has feathers and hatches out of a hard-shelled egg, it's a bird. All birds have wings, and most of them can fly.

● If an animal has six legs and three parts to its body, it's an insect. There are more kinds of insect in the world than all the other kinds of animal put together.

Abdomen

Head

Thorax

● If an animal has damp slimy skin, and is born in water but lives much of its life on land, it's an amphibian. Baby amphibians hatch out of jelly-like eggs.

● If an animal has a dry scaly skin and is born on land, it's a reptile. Most reptiles lay eggs with leathery skins.

Scaly skin

Fin

● If an animal lives in water, breathing through gills and using fins to move, it's a fish. Most fish lay jelly-like eggs which hatch into baby fish.

Gills

257

What's the difference between frogs and toads?

Frogs usually have smooth skin and long legs for leaping. Most toads have lumpy skin and move their short thick bodies about by crawling.

Toad

Frog

...and alligators and crocodiles?

Crocodiles have longer, more pointed snouts than alligators. Crocodiles also have one very large tooth sticking up on each side when they close their mouths.

- Frogs and toads are both amphibians.

- Alligators and crocodiles are reptiles.

Crocodile

Alligator

...and between monkeys and apes?

The big difference between these animals is that monkeys have long tails, but apes don't have tails at all. There are lots of different kinds of monkey, but the only apes are gorillas, orang-utans, chimpanzees and gibbons.

Spider monkey

Orang-utan (ape)

• Monkeys and apes are mammals

• A woodlouse looks like it's an insect, but it isn't – it has too many legs! This creepy-crawly is related to crabs and lobsters.

• Rabbits and hares are both mammals.

...and rabbits and hares?

Hares have longer legs and ears than rabbits. Their whiskers are longer, too.

Why do animals have skeletons inside their bodies?

Not all animals have skeletons, but most large ones do. This is because the bigger an animal is, the more it needs a strong sturdy framework to hold its body together and carry its weight. Skeletons also protect soft inside parts, like brains and hearts.

Backbone

● Animals without backbones are called invertebrates. Insects, spiders, snails, worms, jellyfish, prawns and crabs are all invertebrates.

● Animals with backbones are called vertebrates. Fish are vertebrates, and so are amphibians, reptiles, birds and mammals.

Backbone

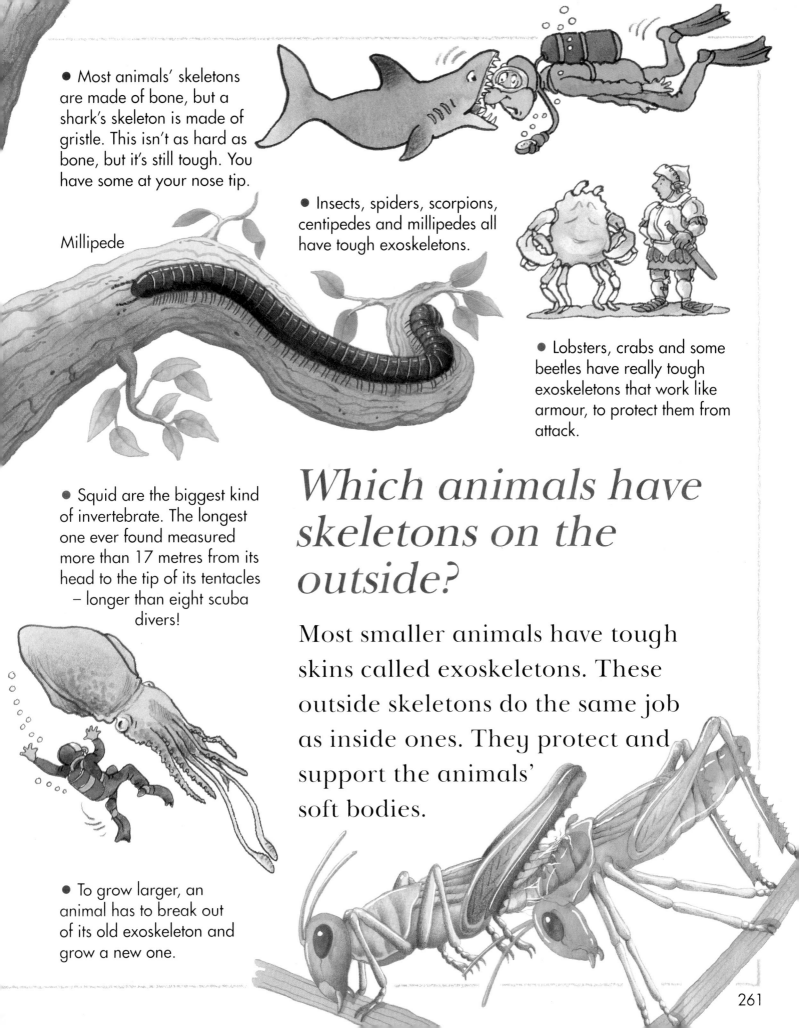

• Most animals' skeletons are made of bone, but a shark's skeleton is made of gristle. This isn't as hard as bone, but it's still tough. You have some at your nose tip.

Millipede

• Insects, spiders, scorpions, centipedes and millipedes all have tough exoskeletons.

• Lobsters, crabs and some beetles have really tough exoskeletons that work like armour, to protect them from attack.

Which animals have skeletons on the outside?

Most smaller animals have tough skins called exoskeletons. These outside skeletons do the same job as inside ones. They protect and support the animals' soft bodies.

• Squid are the biggest kind of invertebrate. The longest one ever found measured more than 17 metres from its head to the tip of its tentacles – longer than eight scuba divers!

• To grow larger, an animal has to break out of its old exoskeleton and grow a new one.

261

When do animals like going to the zoo?

In the past, zoos kept animals just for people to look at. To some people, the animals looked cramped and lonely. Today, many zoos are working hard to breed endangered animals, such as tamarins, and hopefully return them to the wild. If animals could talk, they might say they preferred this kind of zoo.

When do animals like leaving the zoo?

The last wild Arabian oryx was shot in 1972. Luckily, a few were rescued in time and were kept in zoos. They bred well and now a herd of over 100 roams the deserts of Oman once more.

● Sixty-five years ago, the golden hamster was nearly extinct. Then one female and her 12 young were caught and allowed to breed in safety. Soon there were millions of them!

Which endangered animal is brought up in a bucket?

Baby Kemp's ridley turtles are being raised in special hatcheries in the United States and Mexico. In their buckets, they are safe from seabirds and other hunters. When they are big enough to fend for themselves they are put into the ocean.

● Everyone thought the bridled nailtail wallaby, or flashjack, was extinct. Then a colony was discovered in 1973 near Dingo in eastern Australia. The area where they live is now protected.

263

Why do animals need us?

In most cases, animals become endangered because of things that people do. Animals cannot speak so they need some of us to speak up for them. And then they need us to stop doing the bad things we do and save them.

● Lots of people are helping animals in danger. If there's an an oil spill, for example, teams work hard to clean the animals so that they can be returned to the wild.

● Everyone can help to save endangered animals. We can join groups that are trying to protect them. We can be careful about the things we buy, and we can take less from the natural world and make less mess.

Why do we need animals?

Some wild animals provide us with food, clothing and other materials. If they disappear, we'll lose those things. Some animals may be useful to us in ways we don't yet know. Also, animals make the world a beautiful and interesting place. If we lose them, it shows how little we care – for them, for the world and for ourselves.

● Many people believe we should save animals just because they exist. Animals have as much right to be on this planet as we do, and we should treat them with the same kindness as we'd wish for ourselves.

What's it like at the Poles?

The North and South Poles are at the very ends of the Earth. They are freezing cold places with biting winds. Ice and snow stretch as far as the eye can see – not the best place for a holiday!

• Polar bears live at the North Pole, and penguins live at the South Pole. They never get the chance to meet!

• Antarctica is a huge ice-covered continent around the South Pole. In places, the ice is nearly 5 kilometres thick.

Which is the coldest place in the world?

Vostok Station is a really chilly spot in Antarctica. The temperature here is usually about -58 °C, but it has dropped to -89 °C – the coldest ever known!

• Mount Erebus must be the warmest spot in Antarctica. It's an active volcano!

Where do polar bears live?

Polar bears live around the Arctic Ocean, near the North Pole. Funnily enough, they've never lived in Antarctica, though there's plenty of food and just as much snow and ice there.

● Icebergs float in the sea. They were once part of rivers of ice called glaciers.

● Polar bears never slip on the ice. The rough skin and hair on the soles of their feet give them a bit of extra grip.

Why do camels have humps?

A camel's hump is its own built-in food cupboard. By living off the fat stored in its hump, a camel can go for as long as two weeks without eating. Camels need their humps because they live in deserts, where food and water are hard to find.

Why do elephants have trunks?

An elephant's trunk is a helpful tool. It can be used to pull down leaves and branches to eat. It also makes a good hose – elephants can squirt dust or water over themselves to keep cool.

● Elephants say 'hello' to friends by shaking trunks with them.

● An elephant's trunk is a bit like a hand. Using its tip, an elephant can pick up something as small as a button.

- Arabian camels have one hump.

- Bactrian camels have two humps.

- A thirsty camel can drink ten buckets of water in just 10 minutes!

Why do giraffes have long necks?

A giraffe's long neck makes it tall enough to eat the leaves at the top of trees. Other animals cannot reach as high, so the giraffe has lots to eat.

- A giraffe's tongue is half a metre long!

269

How high can a kangaroo hop?

Believe it or not, big kangaroos can hop right over your head! As far as we know, the highest a kangaroo has ever jumped is roughly 3 metres – more than twice as high as you are. Their big strong back legs help kangaroos to be such good high-jumpers.

For their size, fleas are the world's best high-jumpers. They can jump over 100 times their own height.

By hopping in giant leaps, big kangaroos can move nearly as fast as racehorses!

How fast can a cheetah run?

A hungry cheetah can sprint faster than 100 kilometres per hour when chasing something to eat. But running this fast soon wears it out, and it has to stop to get its breath back.

Cheetahs use their sharp claws to grip and push against the ground as they race along. Olympic runners have spikes on their shoes for the same reason.

● Kangaroos use their tails to balance as they hop. They'd probably fall flat on their faces if they didn't.

Which animal has an extra hand?

Some South American monkeys can grip tree branches with just their tails, leaving their hands free to pick fruit and nuts to eat. Unlike most monkeys, whose tails are completely covered with fur, they have bare skin at the end of their tails – rather like the palm of your hand.

● Sloths are very strange slow South American animals. They creep upside down through the treetops, and it can take them a day to move 100 metres!

How many ants can an anteater eat?

On a good day, a giant anteater eats an amazing 30,000 ants! It can scoop up as many as 500 with each flick of its long sticky tongue. Anteaters don't munch their food because they haven't any teeth. They swallow the ants whole.

● Giant anteaters have to walk on the knuckles of their front feet because their claws are so long and sharp. They use these claws to rip ant hills apart.

● Birds that feed on fish often have long sharp beaks. The anhinga uses its beak to spear fish.

● Bears tear bees' nests apart to get at the honey inside. They don't seem to mind getting stung.

Which animal uses its finger as a fork?

A strange monkey-like animal called an aye-aye has one very long thin finger on each hand. It uses these spindly fingers to poke under tree bark for grubs and insects to eat. Then it skewers them, using its fingers a bit like you would use a fork.

● Aye-ayes only live on the island of Madagascar, off the east coast of Africa.

Which is the greediest animal?

For its size, the tiny Etruscan shrew has the world's biggest appetite. It hardly ever stops eating! By the time it's full grown, it has to eat three times its own weight in food each day.

● An adult Etruscan shrew weighs less than a sugar lump.

273

When does a puppy turn into a dog?

Every puppy is blind and helpless when it's born, but by the time it's two years old it will be fully grown. All pups are roughly the same size when they're born, whatever type of dog they are. So it takes smaller breeds less time to finish growing up!

2 By six weeks, the puppy is starting to explore. It plays with its brothers and sisters, and enjoys a tumble!

1 At about two weeks, the puppy's eyes and ears open. It will begin walking soon.

• A baby wildebeest runs before it even walks! The youngster trots along beside its mother just five minutes after it's born.

When does a tiger cub leave home?

A mother tiger looks after her cubs until they're about two years old. But then she has another litter, and ignores the older cubs. It's not really cruel – the two-year-olds are grown-up now, and it's about time they took care of themselves.

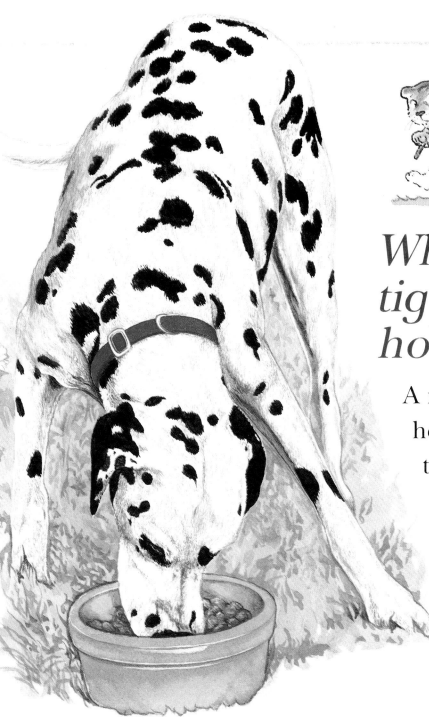

3 By the time it is fully grown, the dog is strong and active. Good food and exercise will help it to stay fit.

Larva

Pupa   **Beetle**

● Most insects change shape as they grow. A beetle starts life as a wriggly larva. Then it turns into a pupa. It may not look like it's doing much, but inside the hard skin the insect is changing fast. When it crawls out, it's a fully-grown beetle.

Which animal is always being washed?

A mother cat licks her kittens from the moment they're born. Licking roughly around the new-born kitten's mouth makes it gasp and start breathing. The mother's tongue dries the kitten's fur too, to keep the kitten warm.

● Flamingos preen their chick's feathers as well as their own. They peck out dirt and insects, and spread oil over the feathers. This oil is produced by the bird's oil glands, and makes the feathers waterproof.

● Mud might not seem a good thing to clean yourself with, but there is nothing a baby hippo likes more than a wallow in a mudbath! Believe it or not, the mud protects the hippo's skin from the sun and keeps it soft.

Who enjoys a good groom?

A baboon makes sure her babies are well groomed. Working slowly, section by section, she parts the baby's fur and picks carefully with her fingers. She will remove pieces of dead skin, insects and dirt – and most of what she finds, she eats!

● Sometimes a foal snaps at its mother, but it's only being friendly! The 'biting' action is the foal's way of asking its mother to nuzzle it and groom its coat.

Which animal lives in the cleanest nest?

Lots of animals keep their babies' nests clean, but the badger would probably win first prize! Adult badgers regularly line their burrows with fresh dried grass and leaves. They even dig special holes well away from the burrow, which the whole family uses as toilets.

W.C.

ENGAGED

Do snakes have good table manners?

Snakes are not polite at mealtimes. They don't chew their meal, they swallow it whole! They stretch their mouth over their food, until it's all gone. And their jaws and body are so elastic that they can eat things much fatter than themselves.

● Snakes can bend and twist because their backbone is made up of hundreds of tiny bones, all linked together like a chain.

● Most snakes are loners, but hundreds of rattlesnakes will snuggle together underground to sleep through the cold winter months.

● An attacking cobra raises its head and spreads out flaps of skin on its head to form a scary-looking hood.

Why do snakes have teeth and fangs?

As well as having teeth to grip their food, poisonous snakes also have a pair of fangs. They use these long teeth to strike their prey and inject them with poison, which shoots out of holes at the tip.

● Vipers have extra-long fangs that fold down flat when they're not in use. It's just as well – they wouldn't be able to shut their mouths otherwise!

Why do snakes stare?

Snakes stare because they can't blink. And they can't blink because they have no eyelids. Each eye is covered by a see-through scale that protects the eye. Snakes get brand-new scales each time they shed their skin.

Which lizard looks both ways at once?

A chameleon's eyes swivel like gun turrets, and can even move in different directions. This doubles the lizard's chances of spotting something to eat, and makes it very difficult for a moth to sneak by without being seen!

Why does a snake flick its tongue?

As a snake's tongue darts in and out, it picks up scents in the air. The tongue carries these up to a sensitive area in the roof of the mouth, which tastes the air. It sends messages to the brain, telling it whether a mate, a meal or an enemy is near.

● Alligators are the noisiest reptiles. They don't just 'talk' to each other, they bellow! In the mating season, males make a terrific row as they try to attract females.

● When the cave anole lizard comes out into the sunshine, it closes its eyes and peeps through scales in its lower eyelids. These protect its eyes like a pair of sunglasses!

What use is a hole in the head?

If you're a lizard, a hole in the head is very useful – because it's probably an ear! Most lizards have an ear on each side of their head. It's just an open hole leading down to the eardrum inside. Reptiles' ears don't stick out from their head like ours do. And snakes' ears are hidden inside their heads.

● Rattlesnakes and other pit vipers can hunt in total darkness. They can sense the body heat of a nearby animal, and strike their prey with amazing accuracy.

Whose tongue is longer than its tail?

The chameleon's sticky-tipped tongue isn't just longer than its tail, it's longer than its whole body! The lizard shoots it out in a twinkling and reels it back in with a meal.

Why do lizards lose their tails?

Lizards can snap off their tails when they're being attacked. The dropped tail wriggles, puzzling the enemy, and giving the lizard time to escape. A new tail grows in a few weeks.

Why do geckos lick their eyes?

Most lizards have eyelids to wipe their eyes, but the gecko doesn't. Like a snake, it has a scale across the eye. To keep its eyes moist and squeaky clean, the gecko licks them, using its long tongue like a handy wipe.

● Most lizards are land-lubbers. The marine iguana from the Galápagos Islands is the only one that lives in the sea.

Are there still dragons on Earth?

The Komodo dragon may not have wings or breathe fire, but it is truly awesome. It's the world's largest lizard – longer than a car, and heavier than a couple of prize-fighters. When people first saw one about 100 years ago, they thought they were looking at a dragon!

Which reptile has a frightful frill?

If you frighten an Australian frilled lizard, it will try to frighten you back. It has a frill of skin around its neck, which it can open up like an umbrella. This makes the lizard look twice its real size. And when it stretches its mouth wide-open too, it's a pretty terrifying sight!

● Steer clear of the horned toad from the United States. It isn't really a toad, it's a lizard, and it can squirt jets of blood – from its eyes! Scary!

● The African pancake tortoise is well named. It's flat enough to wriggle down a crack in a rock. But then it cleverly puffs itself up, so no enemy can tug it out!

Which turtle kicks up a stink?

The stinkpot turtle of the United States has earned its name! When it feels threatened, it lets out a yucky smell that quickly drives away its enemies. And they don't come back!

● The stumpy-tailed skink has a stumpy tail the same shape as its head. As long as it keeps its mouth shut, its enemies can't tell whether the lizard is coming or going!

Why do some snakes pretend to be dead?

Some snakes face danger by pretending that they're dead. The European grass snake rolls on its back, and lies quite still with its mouth open and its tongue hanging out. The enemy probably won't fancy dead snake for lunch and will leave it alone. Then the clever snake comes back to life and makes its escape.

Which reptile is a living fortress?

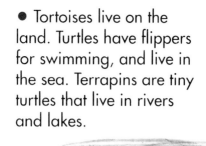

● Tortoises live on the land. Turtles have flippers for swimming, and live in the sea. Terrapins are tiny turtles that live in rivers and lakes.

Living inside a shell is like living inside a fortress. At the first sign of danger, a tortoise retreats inside the shell's thick walls, blocking the 'doors' with its feet and claws. It's well protected from attack, and heat and cold too.

● A tortoise could never park its shell and leave it behind. The shell's horny plates are joined to the skeleton underneath.

Do turtles have teeth?

Turtles don't have teeth, but their horny beaks have plenty of bite. Alligator snapping turtles are particularly fierce. One bite from them, and you could lose your toes!

● A tortoise's damaged shell will slowly heal. A vet can help by patching it with fibreglass, a light material used to build boats.

Which turtle breathes through a snorkel?

The spiny soft-shelled turtle spends most of its time under water in rivers and ponds. It doesn't need to come up to the surface to breathe. It pokes its long snout out of the water like a snorkel, and draws in a noseful of air.

● Turtles were swimming in the ocean more than 200 million years ago. They're the most ancient of all reptiles.

● A tortoise's shell keeps out most enemies, but eagles and vultures have cracked the problem. They drop the poor animals from a great height and smash their shell.

Do reptiles have skin like ours?

A reptile's skin is quite tough and horny, more like our fingernails than our skin. On snakes and lizards, most of the skin is covered with small scales that overlap one another. But crocodiles and turtles have an even tougher skin, with hard plates rather than scales.

● Snakes don't feel slimy. They're dry, cool and pleasant to touch.

● A reptile's scaly skin holds in water, and stops the animal from drying out. This is useful if you live in the desert, as many lizards do.

• A snake's old skin begins to split at the lips. The snake wriggles out head first, turning the skin inside out as it goes. The skin often comes off in one piece, in a perfect snake shape.

Why do snakes shed their skin?

Like your old clothes, a snake's skin wears out and needs replacing – often in a bigger size. So from three to seven times a year, the old skin splits open and peels off, and – hey presto! – there's a brand-new skin waiting underneath.

• In times of danger, the armadillo lizard turns into an armoured ball. It rolls on its back, grips its tail in its mouth and hides its soft belly behind a wall of scales and spines.

Why do some lizards have horns and spikes?

Horns and spikes are a good way of protecting an animal. Like a strong suit of armour, they make a lizard look fierce – and they also make a prickly mouthful for any animal that tries to attack.

Why do birds have feathers?

Feathers keep birds warm. They also help them to fly, by giving their wings and bodies a special sleek shape.

Each kind of bird has feathers of a different colour and pattern. Males are often brighter than females – their good looks help them to attract a mate!

● Birds' fluffy down feathers trap warm air next to their skin – in much the same way as a duvet keeps you warm in bed.

● Hummingbirds are among the world's smallest birds. The bee hummingbird lays its eggs in a nest the size of a walnut.

Which bird can fly backwards?

Hummingbirds are the helicopters of the bird world. They can fly in all directions – backwards, forwards, sideways, up and down. They can even hover on one spot.

● Birds can fly by flapping their wings up and down, or by gliding on still, outstretched wings.

Why can't penguins fly?

Penguins can't fly because their wings are too small to keep their heavy bodies up in the air. But penguins are very good swimmers and divers. They use their wings as paddles in the water.

● Most birds can fold their wings up close to their bodies. But penguins can't. They always hold their wings stiffly out to the side.

● Ostriches are too big to fly, but they can run at twice the speed of the fastest Olympic runners.

What's inside a bird's egg?

There are three things inside a bird's egg – a baby bird, a yellow yolk and a clear jelly called the white. The yolk is food for the growing bird. The white is food, too, but it also protects the bird if the egg gets a knock.

- Some eggs don't get the chance to hatch. They are eaten by hungry hunters.

Why do birds turn their eggs?

Birds turn their eggs so that every part of the egg gets its fair share of warmth. The baby birds need warmth to grow – that's why a parent has to sit on the nest.

ANIMALS
VOLUME II

Which is the biggest creepy-crawly?

The Indonesian giant stick insect is the longest creepy-crawly in the world. At 33 centimetres long, it would only just fit inside the open pages of this book!

Goliath beetle

● The heavyweight champion of the creepy-crawly world is the Goliath beetle. It's as heavy as a hamster.

● Monarch butterflies hold the world record for long-distance flying. Each year they fly from Canada down to Mexico – a journey of over 3,500 kilometres.

MEXICO

● The tropical cockroach is the fastest-known runner in the insect world. It speeds along at over 5 kilometres an hour.

Indonesian giant stick insect

Which is the smallest creepy-crawly?

● Before the time of the dinosaurs, monster-sized dragonflies cruised through the air. Some were the size of seagulls!

You'd find it hard to see a fairy fly, because it's no bigger than a full stop. The female lays her tiny eggs inside the eggs of other insects. She can squeeze as many as 20 into just one butterfly egg.

● The Hercules emperor moth is the world's widest creepy-crawly. From wing to wing, it's the size of a dinner plate!

What is an insect?

An insect has three pairs of legs (that's six altogether), and three parts to its body. The first part is the head, the second is the thorax, and the third is the abdomen.

- Like all insects, this hoverfly has three pairs of legs and three parts to its body.

Feeler

Head

Eye

Thorax

Mouth

Leg

- Woodlice aren't insects. They belong to the same family as crabs, lobsters and shrimps. They don't get together very often though, as woodlice live on land, not in water.

When is a fly not a fly?

A true fly, such as a housefly, has only one pair of wings. Butterflies, dragonflies, damselflies, and mayflies all have two pairs of wings. So they're not really flies at all!

Wing

What is a bug?

Bugs are insects that have needle-like beaks. A bug uses its beak to cut open its food. Then it sucks up the tasty juices inside, using its beak like a straw.

● Bedbugs are the draculas of the insect world. At night, they look for sleeping humans to bite. Then they suck up the tasty blood!

● Centipedes have too many legs to be insects. One kind has 176 pairs!

Abdomen

● There are over a million kinds of insect – more than any other kind of animal in the world. And scientists are still finding new ones!

Are spiders insects?

No – a spider has eight legs, not six. What's more, its body has two parts instead of three. This is because the head and thorax are joined on a spider's body.

Why do spiders spin webs?

A spider's sticky web is its home and its larder!
When an insect flies into the web, it gets stuck. The spider rushes out to spin silk around it. Inside the silk, the insect turns into a liquid mush. Later the spider can suck it up like a drink!

● Most of the webs you see are round orb webs, spun by garden spiders. Other spiders spin webs with different patterns.

How do spiders make thread?

Spiders make runny silk inside their bodies, drawing it out through little knobs called spinnerets. The runny silk sets into thread, which the spider then weaves into a web, using its spinnerets like fingers.

● A Frenchman once took up spider farming. He soon gave the idea up, but not before he managed to make some spider-silk stockings and gloves.

● All spiders spin silk, but they don't all make webs. The spitting spider catches insects by spitting a sticky gum all over them.

When do spiders fly?

When baby spiders hatch out of their eggs, they spin themselves a long, silk line. Then they wait for the breeze to carry them off through the air to new homes, which may be many hundreds of kilometres away.

What does an insect feel with its feelers?

Insects use their feelers to taste and smell – the longer the feelers, the better. Some insects also use their feelers like fingers, to check things out by touching.

Luna moth

● The male luna moth's feelers are long and feathery. He uses them to smell out female moths many kilometres away.

● A male insect's feelers are often larger than a female's. They help him to sniff her out at mating time.

● The cockchafer beetle always fans out its feelers before it flies. They tell it which way the wind is blowing.

Banded longhorn beetle

Cockchafer beetle

● The banded longhorn beetle doesn't just have stripey feelers. The rest of it is blue and black, too!

Ant

Which insect tastes with its toes?

Most insects taste food with their mouths, as we do, but the honey bee can taste with its feet as well. It only needs to land on a flower to sample the dish of the day!

● Spiders have eight eyes, but they're very short-sighted!

Which insect listens with its legs?

The long-horned grasshopper has ears on both its front legs. Its ears don't look like ours, of course. They're tiny holes with skin stretched over the top – a bit like miniature drums.

Why do caterpillars change into butterflies?

Every butterfly has to go through four different stages of its life before it is a fully grown adult. At each stage, it changes its size, its shape and its colour.

● Many kinds of insect change shape as they grow. This way of growing is called metamorphosis.

1 A butterfly lays its eggs on a plant the baby caterpillars eat.

2 The caterpillars eat hungrily, and grow very quickly.

● The babies that hatch from an insect's eggs are known as larvae – but many people just call them grubs.

● Caterpillars grow so quickly that their skin pops open. Underneath, there's brand new skin with plenty of growing room.

3 Each caterpillar makes itself a hard case called a pupa. Inside, its body turns into a kind of mushy soup.

● The pupa is like a strongbox. It keeps the insect's body safe while it changes shape.

NO ENTRY REBUILDING WORK IN PROGRESS

● Nymphs split their skins as they grow, but they don't make a pupa. They just slowly change into adults.

● Not all insects change completely as they grow. A grasshopper's eggs hatch out into tiny nymphs, which look almost like their parents.

● A female butterfly lays as many as 50,000 eggs in her lifetime.

4 The soup slowly turns into a butterfly. When the butterfly wriggles out of the pupa, its wings are soft and creased. They dry in the sunlight.

● Butterflies don't need food to grow, but they love to sip sweet nectar from a flower now and then. It's a fuel that helps them to fly.

Which insects wear armour?

Beetles have two pairs of wings, but they only use one pair to fly. The other pair is like a thick piece of armour, covering the beetle's delicate wings and soft body.

1 When a beetle is scuttling along the ground, its flying wings are hidden beneath a shiny armoured wing casing.

2 When it wants to fly, a beetle opens its armour casing and stretches out its wings.

△ It's not difficult to guess how the giraffe weevil got its name. Its neck is twice as long as its body!

Which beetle fires a spray gun?

Watch out for the bombardier beetle! It shoots its enemies with a jet of hot, stinging liquid. As the jet is fired, it makes a sharp cracking sound like a tiny gun going off.

What digs graves, then robs them?

Burying beetles have no respect for the dead! When they find a dead animal, they dig away the soil until the body sinks into the ground. Then they lay their eggs inside the body and cover it with soil. When the eggs hatch out, there's a tasty, well-stocked meat store waiting for them!

● Imagine rolling balls of snow to make a snowman. That's how scarab beetles roll their balls of animal dung. They push the balls into a safe hiding place, and eat them later on.

● Ancient Egyptians thought the Sun was rolled across the sky by a giant scarab beetle.

3 The beetle beats its wings and moves smoothly through the air.

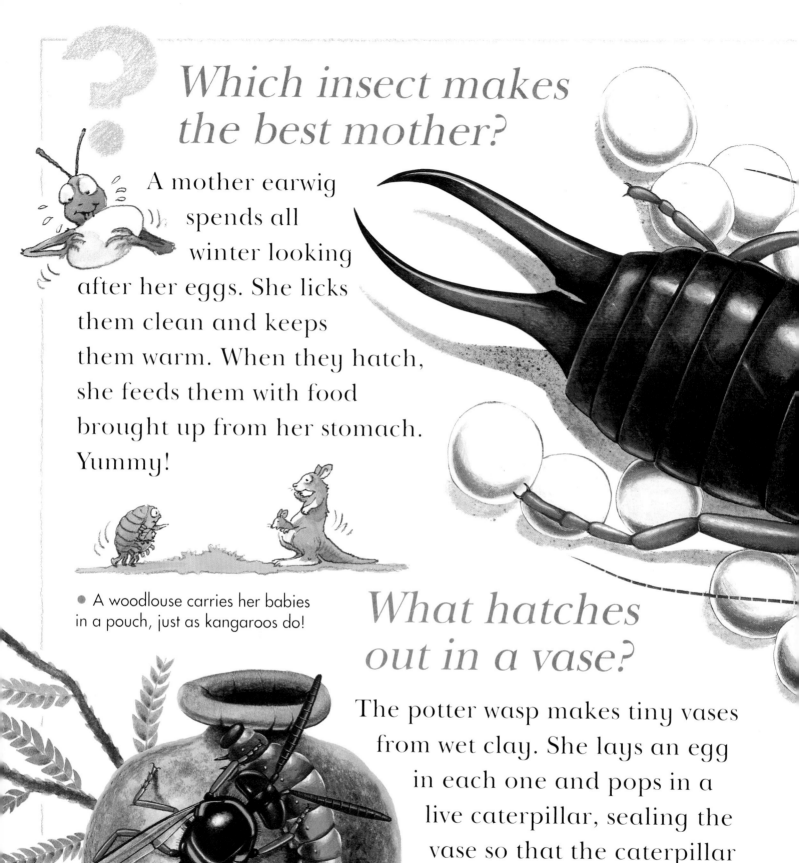

Which insect makes the best mother?

A mother earwig spends all winter looking after her eggs. She licks them clean and keeps them warm. When they hatch, she feeds them with food brought up from her stomach. Yummy!

● A woodlouse carries her babies in a pouch, just as kangaroos do!

What hatches out in a vase?

The potter wasp makes tiny vases from wet clay. She lays an egg in each one and pops in a live caterpillar, sealing the vase so that the caterpillar can't escape. When the baby wasp hatches out, its first meal is waiting for it!

Which insect is the laziest parent?

The cuckoo bee doesn't look after her own babies. Instead, she sneaks into another bee's nest and lays her eggs there. When the baby cuckoo bees hatch out, they eat any food they find – even their foster brothers and sisters!

● A queen bee lays up to 3,500 eggs a day, for several weeks at a time. No wonder she only lives for a couple of years!

● The larvae of the phantom midge float in the water on little pockets of air.

● The wolf spider carries her eggs around in a silk backpack. When the babies hatch out, they climb out on to her back and ride piggyback.

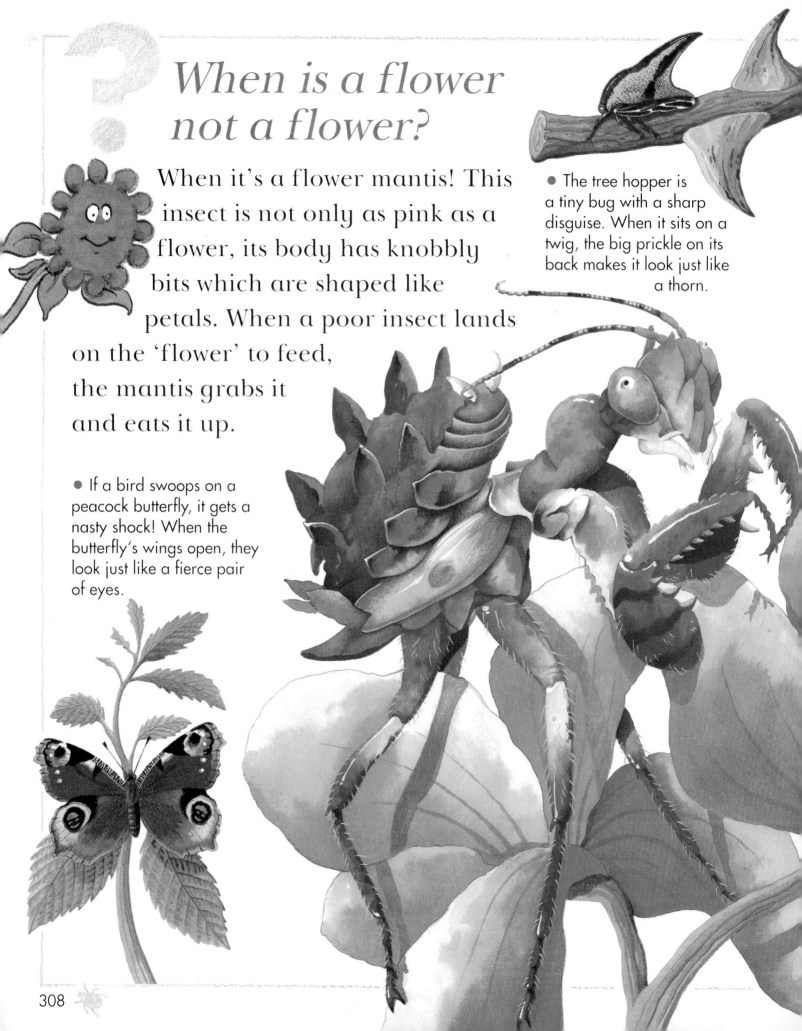

When is a flower not a flower?

When it's a flower mantis! This insect is not only as pink as a flower, its body has knobbly bits which are shaped like petals. When a poor insect lands on the 'flower' to feed, the mantis grabs it and eats it up.

● The tree hopper is a tiny bug with a sharp disguise. When it sits on a twig, the big prickle on its back makes it look just like a thorn.

● If a bird swoops on a peacock butterfly, it gets a nasty shock! When the butterfly's wings open, they look just like a fierce pair of eyes.

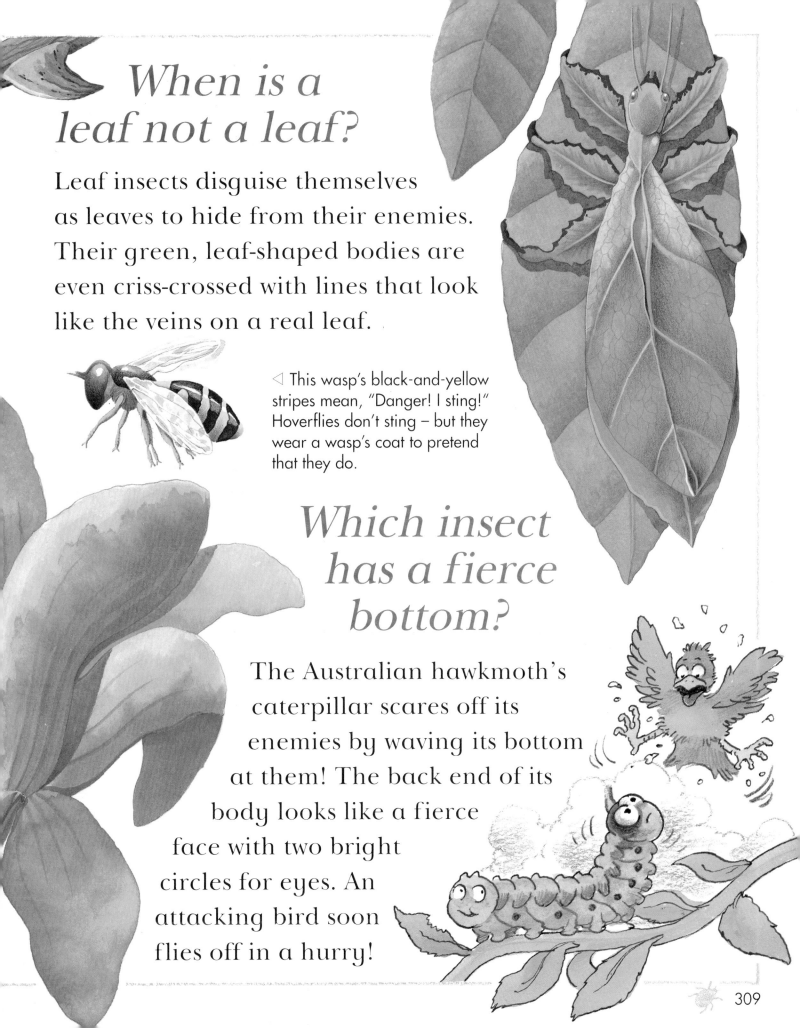

When is a leaf not a leaf?

Leaf insects disguise themselves as leaves to hide from their enemies. Their green, leaf-shaped bodies are even criss-crossed with lines that look like the veins on a real leaf.

◁ This wasp's black-and-yellow stripes mean, "Danger! I sting!" Hoverflies don't sting – but they wear a wasp's coat to pretend that they do.

Which insect has a fierce bottom?

The Australian hawkmoth's caterpillar scares off its enemies by waving its bottom at them! The back end of its body looks like a fierce face with two bright circles for eyes. An attacking bird soon flies off in a hurry!

Why do bees live in hives?

In the wild, families of honey bees live in holes in a tree or a rock. But if a friendly beekeeper provides a couple of cosy hives, then the bees are very happy to move in. This is really to help the beekeeper, of course – collecting honey from a hive is much easier than climbing a tree!

● When beekeepers open a hive, they wear special overalls, gloves and veils to protect themselves from bee stings.

Why do bees dance?

When a honey bee finds plenty of food, it flies back to the hive to tell its friends. It does this by dancing. The number of wiggles in the dance, and the direction the bee points, tell the other bees exactly where to go.

● Bees not only have a brush, they have a comb! It's on their front legs, and they use it to clean their feelers.

● Collecting nectar to make honey is hard work. A bee would have to make 10 million trips to get enough for a single jar!

Why do bees carry brushes and baskets?

Honey bees have little baskets on their back legs and brushes of hair on their other legs. When a bee lands on a flower, it brushes a powder called pollen into its baskets. Then it flies back to the hive to feed the pollen to its young.

● Bears rob honey from bees' nests. Their thick fur protects them from bee stings – except on the nose!

● Not all bees like to live in hives. Many kinds of bee live alone, in burrows.

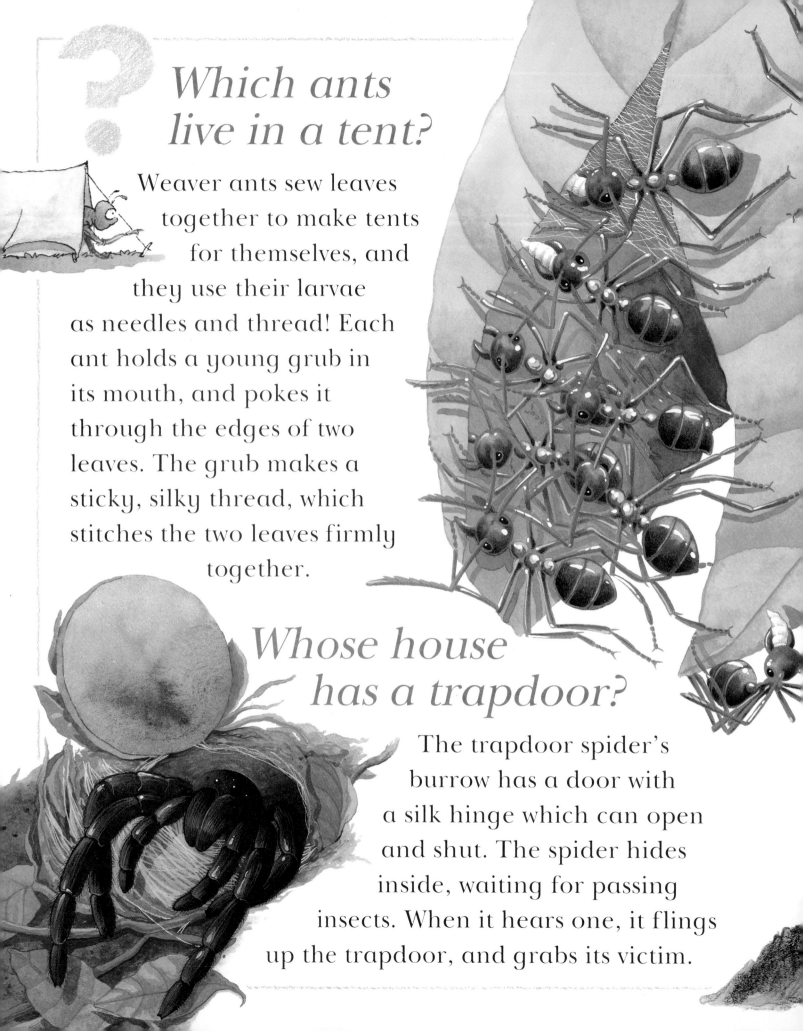

Which ants live in a tent?

Weaver ants sew leaves together to make tents for themselves, and they use their larvae as needles and thread! Each ant holds a young grub in its mouth, and pokes it through the edges of two leaves. The grub makes a sticky, silky thread, which stitches the two leaves firmly together.

Whose house has a trapdoor?

The trapdoor spider's burrow has a door with a silk hinge which can open and shut. The spider hides inside, waiting for passing insects. When it hears one, it flings up the trapdoor, and grabs its victim.

● Many creepy-crawlies make their homes in your home. Ants, spiders, moths, centipedes and houseflies all like to live indoors.

Whose nest is paper thin?

The paper wasp's nest has paper walls. It makes the paper by chewing up strips of wood, which it tears from plants or old fence posts! It spreads the mixture in thin layers to build the nest.

● A tent caterpillar spins a shady silk canopy, and shelters under it while it feeds.

● Termites are champion builders, and make mud nests up to four times taller than a man. They need the room – as many as 5 million termites may be living inside!

What has a sting in its tail?

A scorpion attacks by curving its tail over its head. It stabs its prey with the sharp end of its tail, and then squirts out poison. Ouch!

Can spiders kill people?

Although spider bites can hurt a lot, very few are poisonous enough to kill you. The black widow is the best-known deadly spider. Her poison is powerful enough to kill a human. She has another nasty habit, too – sometimes she eats her mate!

● The poison of a black widow spider is 15 times deadlier than a rattlesnake's.

What kills over a million people a year?

In some hot countries, mosquitoes carry a deadly illness called malaria. They can pass this on to anyone they bite. Over 200 million people catch malaria every year, and more than a million die from it.

● Doctors have cures for most spider bites, but they need to know exactly which spider's poison they are treating. So if you're ever bitten by a spider, remember to ask it its name!

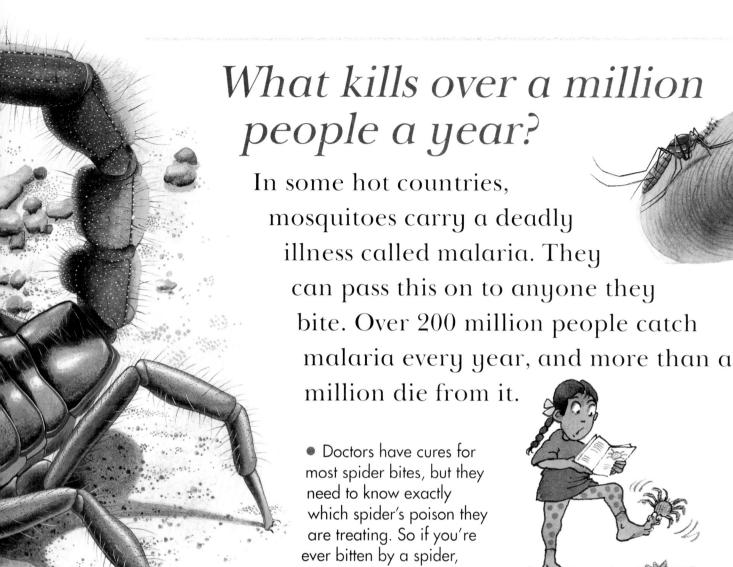

Which killing machine has 120 million legs?

A swarm of army ants can be up to 20 million strong. The ants have no home, but live on the move, eating anything that gets in their way – and that can include people!

315

Are creepy-crawlies good for people?

Most creepy-crawlies are harmless – and some of them are valuable friends. They help plants to grow, keep the Earth clean, and give us useful things such as silk to wear and honey to eat.

- People who study insects are called entomologists. They travel all around the world, learning about insects and trying to protect them.

- How would you feel about eating a toasted grasshopper? In different parts of the world, grasshoppers, locusts and caterpillars are served as tasty titbits.

- Insects are the world's rubbish collectors, cleaning up mucky things like dung and dead bodies.

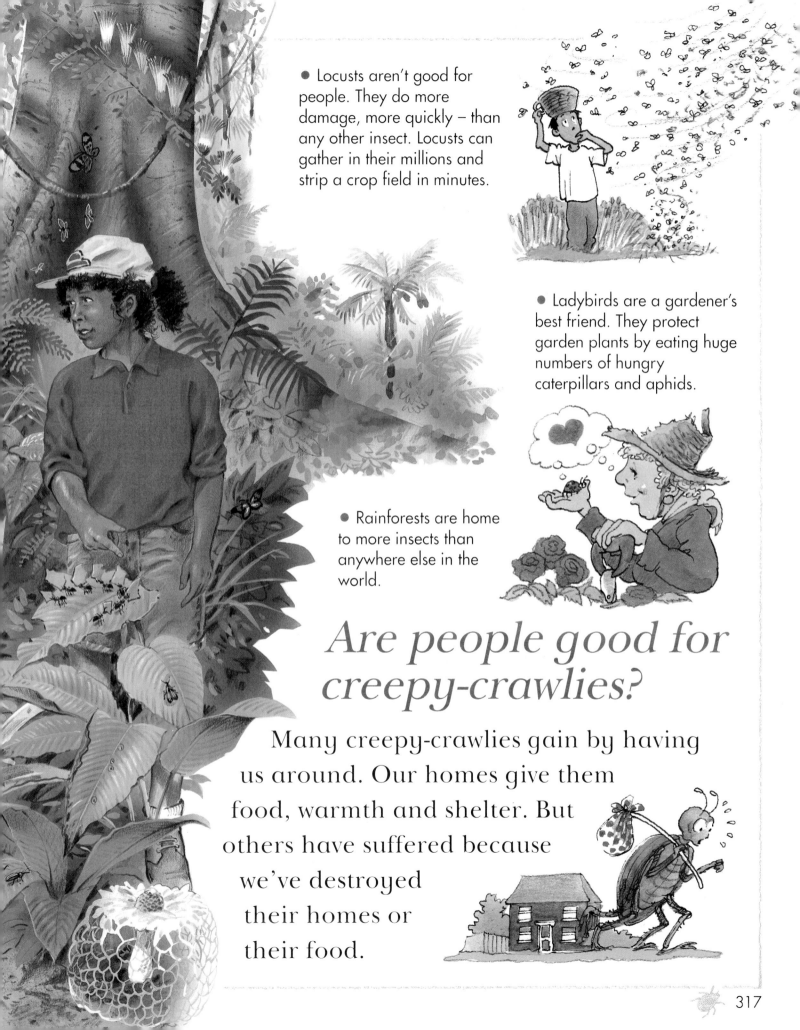

● Locusts aren't good for people. They do more damage, more quickly – than any other insect. Locusts can gather in their millions and strip a crop field in minutes.

● Ladybirds are a gardener's best friend. They protect garden plants by eating huge numbers of hungry caterpillars and aphids.

● Rainforests are home to more insects than anywhere else in the world.

Are people good for creepy-crawlies?

Many creepy-crawlies gain by having us around. Our homes give them food, warmth and shelter. But others have suffered because we've destroyed their homes or their food.

Which is the biggest fish?

The whale shark is the world's biggest fish. It's gigantic – as long as eight scuba divers lying head to toe, and as heavy as six large elephants.

● The dwarf goby is the smallest fish in the ocean.

● The oar fish is the longest fish in the ocean – as long as four canoes placed end to end.

Oar fish

● The biggest sea plant is the giant kelp seaweed. A single strand can grow nearly as long as a football pitch!

Sailfish

Which is the fastest fish?

The sailfish can race along under water at over 100 kilometres an hour – as fast as a car. It tucks its fins in tightly, and its pointed nose cuts through the water like a knife.

Whale shark

Which is the biggest crab?

● The pea-sized pea crab is the smallest crab of all. It lives inside oyster and mussel shells.

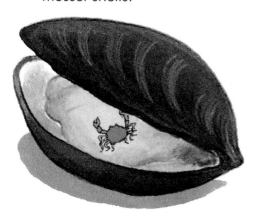

Japan's giant spider crab measures nearly 4 metres from the tip of one front claw to the tip of the other. It could open its arms wide enough to hug a hippopotamus!

How do fish breathe under water?

▷ Not all sea creatures can breathe under water. Sea cows, seals and dolphins breathe air, so they have to keep coming to the surface.

Fish have to breathe to stay alive, just as you do. But while you breathe oxygen from the air, fish take it from water. As they swim, fish gulp in water and push it out through slits called gills on their heads.

Oxygen passes from the water into the fish's blood inside their gills.

Gill cover

Fish swim by using their muscles to ripple their bodies along. Wiggling their tails from side to side gives them extra push. They use their other fins to balance and change direction.

Which bird flies under water?

Penguins can't fly through the air because their wings are too short and stumpy. They are much more at home in the ocean, where they use their wings as flippers.

• Seahorses aren't strong swimmers. They hang on to seaweed to avoid being swept away.

Which animal is jet-propelled?

Squid don't have flippers or a tail, but they're still fast movers. They suck water into their bodies, then squirt it out so powerfully that their bodies shoot backwards.

• Squid have ten tentacles – that's two more than their relative, the octopus.

Which fish has headlights?

It's so dark at the bottom of the ocean that some fish make their own light. The angler fish has a long fin dangling in front of its face. At the end of the fin is a blob which glows. Small fish are drawn towards the glowing light, only to disappear into the angler fish's big, gaping mouth.

● The deep sea is inky black and as cold as a fridge. Even so, some amazing creatures live there.

Angler fish

How deep is the ocean?

● The seabed has huge cracks in it, called trenches. Some are over 10 kilometres deep.

Away from the shore, the ocean plunges to about 4 kilometres in most places. That's deep enough to swallow Ben Nevis, Britain's tallest mountain, three times!

Gulper eel

Are there worms under the sea?

Lots of types of worm live in the sea. Giant red-and-white tube worms live near holes in the seabed, called vents. These spurt out boiling water – so they're one of the few places in the deep where it's warm.

● Many deep-sea fish are real ugly mugs. It's just as well it's so dark down there!

● Hot water from the vents warms the seabed and helps bacteria to grow – which makes yummy food for the tube worms!

Dragonfish

Where do angels, clowns and parrots live?

Angelfish, clownfish and parrotfish are just some of the thousands of beautiful animals that live on coral reefs. Tropical fish like these often have dazzling colours and bold patterns.

Imperial angelfish

Parrotfish

• Coral reefs grow in shallow water in the warmest parts of the world.

Angelfish

• Giant clams live on coral reefs. Their shells are big enough to have a bath in!

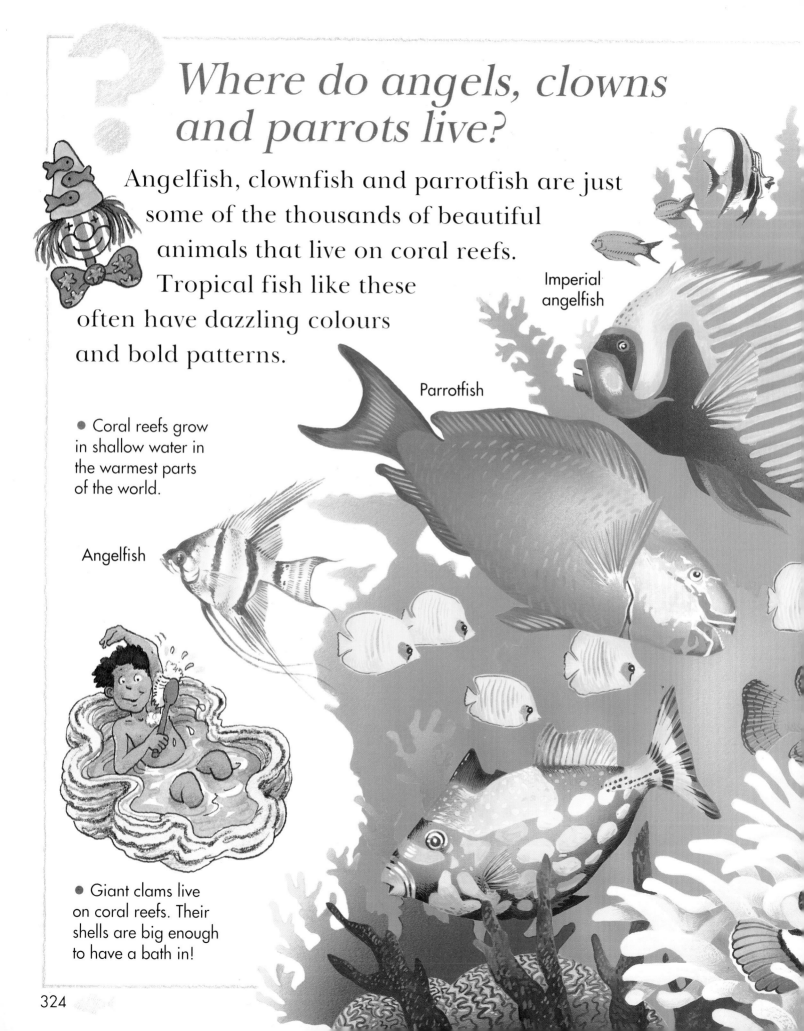

What is a coral reef?

● Corals comes in all sorts of shapes – antlers, plates, mushrooms, feathers, daisies and even brains!

A coral reef is like a beautiful underwater hedge. It looks stony and dead – but it is really alive! Coral is made up of millions of tiny animals, which leave their hard skeletons behind when they die. Each new layer piles on to the old, slowly building the coral rock.

Where is the biggest reef?

The world's biggest coral reef lies in warm shallow seas off the northeast coast of Australia. It's called the Great Barrier Reef, and it stretches for more than 2,000 kilometres. It's so huge that it can be seen by astronauts up in space.

Clown fish

325

Which fish hunts with a hammer?

The hammerhead shark has a huge head shaped like a hammer. But this tool is for hunting, not banging in nails. The shark's eyes and nostrils are at each end of the hammer. As the shark swims, it swings its head from side to side, searching for a meal.

● The Portuguese man-of-war catches its tea in its long, stinging tentacles.

Which is the most shocking fish?

Some fish give off electric shocks to protect themselves or to stun animals they want to eat. The most shocking ocean fish is the torpedo ray. If you could switch it on, it would light up a light bulb!

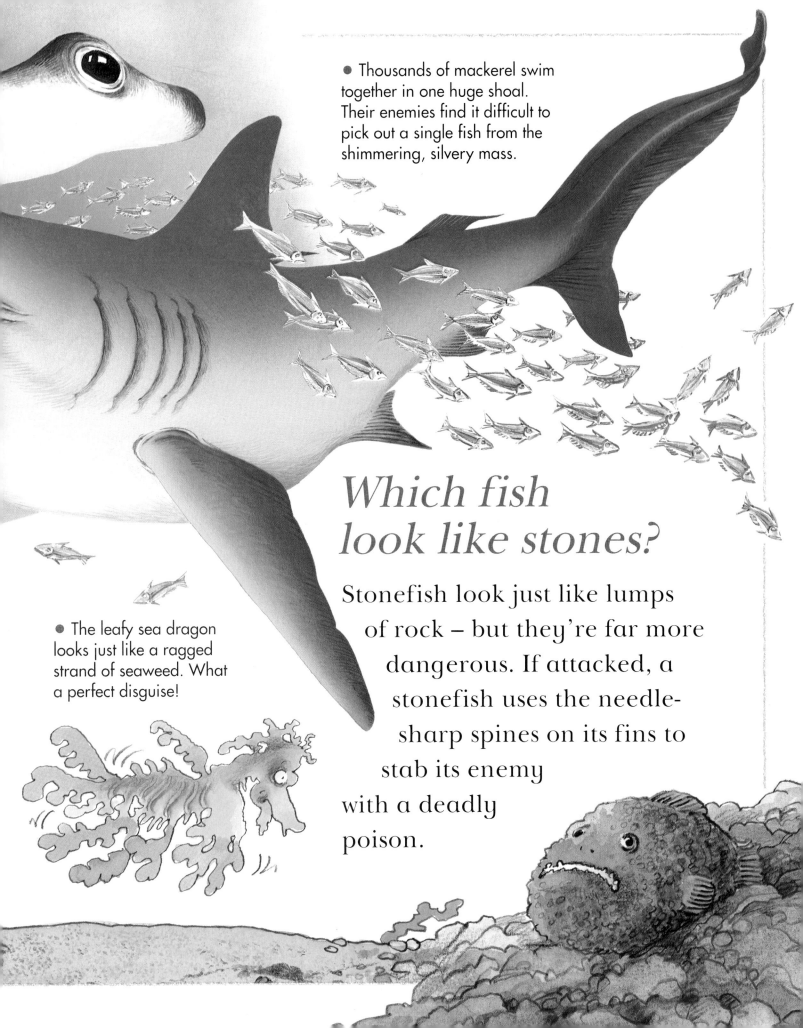

• Thousands of mackerel swim together in one huge shoal. Their enemies find it difficult to pick out a single fish from the shimmering, silvery mass.

Which fish look like stones?

Stonefish look just like lumps of rock – but they're far more dangerous. If attacked, a stonefish uses the needle-sharp spines on its fins to stab its enemy with a deadly poison.

• The leafy sea dragon looks just like a ragged strand of seaweed. What a perfect disguise!

Which animals shoot their food?

If an archer fish spots an insect sitting on a plant above the water, it shoots it – not with an arrow or a bullet, of course, but with a jet of water squirted from its mouth. The insect falls into the water and the fish gobbles it up.

● The bolas spider swings a thread with a sticky blob at the end to catch insects. A bolas is a lasso used by South American cowboys.

● The archer fish is a good shot. It can hit an insect up to 3 metres away from it.

● The sound of the pistol shrimp's big left pincer snapping shut sends shock waves through the water, stunning small fish and making them easier to catch.

Index

This index will help you to find out where you can read information about a subject. It is in alphabetical order. Each section is under a large letter of the alphabet. A main entry and its page numbers are printed in dark, or bold, letters. This is where you will find the most information. Other page numbers show where you can find further information.

A

Afghanistan 225
agriculture 39, 180, 181, **230-231**
air 49, **62**, **72**
aircraft 39, 43, 94, 95, **97-99**, **100**, **110**, 160, **162**
Alaska 224
alligators 258, 281
alpenhorns 247
amphibians 257, 258, 260
Anasazi people 199
Andes Mountains 232
angelfish 324
angler fish 322
anhingas 272
animals 34, 37, 41, 69, 88, 106, 151, 184, **220-221**, 231, 238, 248, **254-293**
   dinosaurs 174-179
Antarctica *see* Polar regions
anteaters 272
ants 272, **312**, 313, **315**
apes 259
Aphrodite 191
Arabian oryx 262
Arabs 197
   Arabic language 226
archaeologists 194-195
archaeopteryx 179
archer fish 328
Arctic *see* Polar regions

armies 181, 189, 201, 205
armour 200-201
astronauts 252
astronomers 15, 17, 23, 29
Athene 190-191
Atlantic Ocean 50, 51
atmosphere 42, 43
Australia 106, 107, **231**, **244**, 263, 309, **325**
aye-ayes 273
Aztecs 136, 137, 201, **207**

B

babies 74-75, 218, **274-277**, **292-293**, 299
baboons 277
badgers 277
bagpipes 245
balloons 101
bar codes 142
barges 251
basketball 156, 157
baths 149
bears 272, 311
bees 301, **307**, **310-311**
beetles 261, 294, 300, **304-305**
bicycles 94, 141, **161-163**, **225**
Big Bang 14-15
birds 34, 99, 113, 179, **257**, 260, 272, **290-293**
biros 165
birth 74-75

black dwarves 21
blood 80-81
boats *see* ships
body, human 72-92
bones 76-77, 179,
  260-261, 325
bongos 240
Borneo 250
Boston Tea Party 211
brain 82-83, 185
breathing 84-85, **320**
bricks 112, 115
bridges 130-132
Britain 124, 128, 130,
  132, **204**, **206**, 208,
  211, 229, **232**
bubbles 63, 71
bugs 297, 308
buildings 112-127,
  186-187, 190, 198-
  199, 209
bulldozers 123
bull-roarers 243
bungee-jumpers 132
butterflies 220, 254,
  293, 294, **302-303**,
  308

C

Caesar, Julius 136
calendars 136-137
camels 248, **268-269**
Canada 126, **202**,
  218, **224**, **230**
cannons 199
carbon dioxide 62, 63
card-playing 158
Caribbean 240

carnivals 239, 240
carpets 149
cars 95, **96**, **102**, **104-
  105**, 111, **160**, 161
cash registers 142
castles 198-199
caterpillars 293, **302-
  303**, **309**, 313, 316
cathedrals 124
cats 69, **276**
CD-ROMs 164
centipedes 261, 297,
  313
chameleons 280, **281**
cheetahs 270
child labour 212
chimpanzees 259
China 41, 103, 143,
  149, **218**, 222, **225**,
  226, **236**
chocolate 231
clams 324
clocks 138-139
clothes 155, 186, 195,
  206, 212, **232-234**,
  265, 299
clouds 44
clownfish 324
coal 212
cobras 279
Coca-Cola 144
cockroaches 294
coconuts 231
colours 69
Columbus, Christopher
  209
comets 24
computers 159, 164,

165, 169, 172
Concorde 98
concrete 116, 118,
  119, 130
constellations 18
continents 34-35
cooking 63, 141, 147
  see also foods
coral reefs 324-325
cornflakes 144
Cortés, Hernan 207
**countries of the world
  214-217**
crabs 260, 261, **319**
cramp 79
crocodiles 258, 288
Crystal Palace 212
cyclists *see* bicycles

D

dancing 247
Demeter 191
demolition 122-123
denim 155
deserts 180, 233, 251,
  262, 268
didgeridoos 244
diggers 116-117
dinosaurs 174-179
divers 109
Diwali 236-237
dogs 274
dolls 159
dolphins 256
dragonflies 295
dress *see* **clothes**
drinking straws 145
drums 241

E

ears **88-89**, 301
Earth 16, 19, 24, **32-52**, 95
earthquakes **40-41**
earwigs **306**
Ecuador 237
eggs **292-293**, 303, 305, 306, 307
Egyptians, Ancient 150, 152, 164, **180-187**, 305
Eiffel Tower 124
Elasmosaurus 179
elastic 155
electricity 105, 147, 326
elephants **238-239**, 254, **268**
Elizabeth I, Queen 207
emus 34
endangered animals **262-265**
energy **56-61**, 104
engines 95, **105**
entomologists 316
equator 221
Esala Perahera **239**
Eurotunnel 128-129
experiments 54-55
explorers 202-203, 209
eyes **86-87**

F

farming see agriculture
faxes 169
festivals **236-239**

fish **257**, 260, 272, 293, **318-328**
fishermen 224
flags **214-215**
flamenco **247**
flamingos 276
fleas 270
flies **295-296**, 313
flower mantis **308**
foods 144, **228-231**, 235, 237, 238, 265
animal 268, 272, 273, 301, 303, 310-311
see also cooking
football **249**
footwear 156
fossils, dinosaur **176-177**
France 124, 126, 128, **205**, **210**, **235**
fridges 144
Frisbees™ 134
frogs **258**, 293

G

galaxies 14, 15-17
gamelan orchestras **242**
gardens 251, 317
geckos **283**
Genghis Khan (Temujin) **205**
Germany 216
germs 92
gibbons 259
giraffes 254, **269**
glass 65

gods/goddesses **190-191**, 241
gorillas 259
governments 214
grasshoppers **301**, 316
Great Barrier Reef **325**
Great Exhibition (1851) 212
Great Zimbabwe 199
Greece **234**
Greeks, Ancient 149, **188-191**
greenhouse effect **42**
Gro-bags™ 151
guillotines 210
Gunpowder Plot 209
guns 199

H

Hades 191
hairdressers 153
hamsters 263
hang-gliders 59
hares 259
hats **232**
Hawaii 37, 44, 52
head, human **82-83**
hearing **88-89**
heart **80-81**
heat 18, 22-23, 26, 42, **58-59**
Hebrew languuage 226
helium 18, 100
Henry VIII, King 206
Hera 191
Hermes 191
hiccups **85**

Himalayas 36-7, 222
Hindus 227, 234, **236-237**
hippopotamuses 276
Homer 191
honey 310-311, 316
horses 149, 151, 277
housing 112-116, 250-252, 313, 317
hovercraft 109, **160**
hoverflies 309
Hubble Space Telescope 29
human beings 74-92, 255, 264-265, 314, 315, 317
hummingbirds 290
hurricanes 48
hydrogen 18
hydroplanes 96

I

Ibn Batuta 203
icebergs 267
iceboxes 144, 145
ice-skating 157
illnesses 92, 315
India 209, 221, **233**, 234, **236-237**
Indian Ocean 50, 51
Indonesia 242, 246
industrial revolution 212
insects 70-71, 114, 130, **244, 257**, 260, 261, 270, 275, 293, **294-317**
inventions 134-172, 212

invertebrates 260-261
Iraq 113
Ireland 238
Italy 223, **229**

J

James VI, King of Scotland 207
Japan 126, 167, 201, 224, **226, 229**, 319
jazz 242, 245
jeans 155
jellyfish 260
jet-skis 157
Jewish New Year 237
Jew's harps 244
Joan of Arc 205
jumbo jets 98, 110
Jupiter 24, **28-29**

K

kangaroos 270-271
karate 123
Kenya 245
kilts 232
knights 200-201
knots (speed) 140
Komodo dragons 283
Koran, The 209

L

ladybirds 317
languages 226-227
larvae 302, 307
lawnmowers 151
laws 181, 189
leaf insects 309
leap years 137

Lego 158
Lhasa 222-223
lifts, passenger 125
light 18, 19, **64-69, 72**, 86-7
lightning 46-7
lipsticks 152
lizards 280-284, 288-289
lobsters 261
locks (door) 150
locusts 316, 317
London 132
longhouses 250
Louis XVI, King 210

M

mackerel 327
Madagascar 234, 273
Maglevs 107
malaria 315
mammals 256, 259-277
Maoris 203, **235**
maracas 243
Marco Polo 203
Mars 24, **27**, 252
Meccano™ 158
Mercury 24, 25, 26-7
methane 30
metronomes 141
Mexico 220, **223, 239**, 263
microwave ovens 147
Middle Ages 196-197, 200
midges 307
migration 220

Milky Way **16-17**
millipedes 261
mirlitons 245
mirrors 66
monasteries 206
money 143, 214, 234
Mongols 201, **205, 251**
monkeys 231, **259, 271**
monsoons 221
Moon 34, 97
mosquitoes 315
moths 295, 300, 309, 313
mountain bikes 162
mountains 36-39, 222, 232
mummies, Egyptian 184-185
muscles 78-79, 85, 320
music 60-61, 141, 170-171, 215, **240-245**, 247

N
Native Americans 208-209, 247
Navajo people 247
Neptune 25, 29, 30, **31**
nerves 83, 87-91
Netherlands 251
New England 208
New Year's celebrations 236-237
New Zealand 203,

227, **235**
Nigeria 241
nitrogen 62
noses 90

O
oceans 50-52, 322-323
Odysseus 191
oil 104
optical fibres 169
orang-utans 259
ostriches 254, 291
oxygen 42, 62, 72, 75, **84, 320**
ozone 43

P
Pacific Ocean 50, 51
paddle-steamers 103
Pakistan 149
pancakes 228
Papua New Guinea 227
parrotfish 324
Parthenon 190, 191
pasta 229
pelota 249
penguins 266, **291, 321**
penny-farthings (bicycles) 161
pens 165
periscopes 66
personal stereos 167
petrol 104-105
pharaohs 182-183, 186

Philippines 241
photography 166
piles (foundations) 118-19
Pilgrim Fathers 208-209
planes see aircraft
planets 24-31
plants 64, **72-73**, 135, 318
plasters (surgical) 153
Pluto 25, **30**
pocket calculators 165
Polar bears 267
Polar regions 42, **219, 266-267**
Arctic Ocean 50, 51
Polynesia 203
Pompeii 194-195
Pompidou Centre, Paris 126
pond-skaters 70
Portugal 224
Portuguese man-of-war 326
Poseidon 191
potato crisps 145
prawns 260
puppets 246
PVC 154
pyramids 124, 181, **186-187**

R
rabbits 259
radios 167
rain 44, 70, 221
rainbows **68-69**

raincoats 154
rainforests 317
rattles 243
rattlesnakes 278, 281
rays (fish) 326
razors 153
recording studios 171
red giants 20
reflection 66
reptiles 174-179, 257, 258, 260, 278-289
rice 230
road trains 106
Robin Hood 204
robots 170
roller skating 157
Romans, Ancient 136, 149, 159, 192-196
Rosh Hashanah 237
rubber 135
Russia 219

S

safety pins 135
sailfish 318
sailing craft 96, 203
sailors 139, 140, 197, 203
Saint Patrick 238
salt 210
sandglasses 141
saris 233
Saturn 24, 29
Saudi Arabia 105, 248
scientists 54-55
scorpions 261, 314
Scotland 130, 154, 179, 207, 232-233

screws 150
sea dragons 327
seahorses 321
seas 51, 322-323
seasons 220-221
seaweed 318
seeing 87
shadows 64-65
sharks 255, 256, 261, 318, 326
sheep 231
ships 96, 103, 108-109, 111, 132, 140, 203, 206, 207
shrews 273
shrimps 328
sieges 198
silk 299, 316
Sinbad the Sailor 203
singers 60
skating 157
skeletons 76-77, 179, 260-261, 325
skinks 285
SkyDome stadium, Toronto 126-7
skyscrapers 118-120, 124-125
sloths 271
smell 90
snails 260
snakes 255, 278-280, 281, 285, 288-289, 293
sneezes 85
snow 45, 102, 266-267

snowmobiles 224
soap 71
soldiers see armies
sound 60-61, 88-89
recording 171
space exploration 26, 29, 31, 97, 110, 252
Spain 207
speed 94-95
spiders 260, 261, 293, 297-299, 301, 307, 312, 313, 314, 315, 328
sports 140, 156-157, 249
squid 261, 321
Sri Lanka 238
stadiums 126-7
stamps 214
stars 14, 17-21, 25, 181
steam power 160, 212
steel 118-121, 126
steel bands 240
stick insects 294
stonefish 327
submarines 108-109
Sun 7, 16, 20-1, 22-23, 25, 27, 139
Sun gods 181, 182
sunlight 58-59, 68-69, 72
supermarket trolleys 143
supernovas 21
surface tension 70-71
Switzerland 247
synthesisers 171

T

Taj Mahal 209
taste 91
TBMs (tunnel-boring machines) 128-129
tea 143, 146, 229
teddy-bears 158
teeth 91, 152
Teflon™ **147**
telephones 167, **168-169**
telescopes 29
temples 181, 189, 190
termites 244, 313
Thailand 231
thunderstorms 46-47
Tibet 143, **222-223**
tigers 275
toads 258
toasters 146
toilets 148
tongues 91
tornadoes 48
tortoises 284, **286-287**
Tower Bridge, London 132
toys 158-159
trainers (footwear) 156
trains 95, 106, **107**, 212, 224
trams 107
transport 94-111
tree hoppers 308
triangles (music) 243
tropical lands 221
trucks 106, 111, 123, 225
Tudors 206

tunnels 128-129
Turkey 201, **234**
turtles 263, **284**, **286-287**, 293
TV 166
typewriters 164
tyres 103, 135

U

unicycles 163
universe 14-31
Uranus 25, 29, 30
USA 48, **110**, **125**, 127, 132, 146, **158**, 167, 169, **211**, 218, 223, **230**, **247**

V

Velcro™ fastenings 135
Venice 203, **223**
Venus 24, **26**
vertebrates 260
Vesuvius, Mount 195
videophones 169
Vietnam 246
Vikings 202-203
Vinland 202
vipers 279, 281
virtual reality 172
volcanoes 38-39, **194-195**, 266
Voyager 2 31

W

Wales 201
wallabies 263
walled cities 199

Washington, George 211
wasps 306, 309, **313**
watches 138-139
water 54-55, 61, 67, 70-71, **73**
waves 52
weapons 199, 200-1
weather 44-49, 220-1
weddings 234
whales 61, 72, **254-255**
wheat 230
wheels 102-103
white dwarves 21
wildebeest 221, 274
winds 49, 62
wings 99
woodlice 259, 296, 306
worms 260, 323
wrecking balls 122

Y

yurts 251

Z

zebras 221
Zeus 191
zips 154
zoos 262-263

Acknowledgements

The publishers would like to thank the following
artists for their contribution to this book:

Susanna Addario 166–167, 208–209; **Simone Boni** (Virgil Pomfret Agency) 222–223; **Peter Cornwell** 212;
Joanne Cowne 274–275; **Peter Dennis** (Linda Rogers Associates) 126–127, 154–157, 214–215, 234–235, 238–245;
Micheal Fisher 124–125, 130–131; **Chris Forsey** 14–15, 32–52, 55*br*, 58–59, 62*tl*, 63*tr*, 65*tr*, 67*tr*, 68–73, 76–83,
86–89, 92*tl*, 94–97, 104–107, 112–115, 120–123, 128–129, 132, 162–163, 164*tr*, 168–170, 174–179, 186–187,
196–197, 216–217, 224–227, 230–231, 248–249, 252, 267, 276–277, 282–283, 294–295, 316–319; **Terry Gabbey**
(AFA Ltd) 136–139, 160–161, 198–199, 246–247; **Luigi Galante** (Virgil Pomfret Agency) 180–181, 192–193, 250–251;
Ruby Green 54–55, 62–63, 66–67, 71*br*, 74–75, 92, 150–151, 158–159; **Craig Greenwood** (Wildlife Art Agency)
220–221; **Nick Harris** (Virgil Pomfret Agency) 142–143; **Stephen Holmes** 254–261, 268–273, 290–291, 308–309,
312–313, 328; **Adam Hook** (Linden Artists) 200*tl*; 204*tl*, **Christa Hook** (Linden Artists) 200–201; **Christian Hook** 140–141,
194–195, 210–211, 264–265; **Biz Hull** (Artist Partners) 56–57, 60–61, 64–65, 134–135, 146–147, 164–165, 262–263;
Tony Kenyon (BL Kearley) all cartoons; **Adrian Lascom** (Garden Studio) 296–297, 300–301; **Alan Male** (Linden Artists)
286–287, 304–307, 314–315; **Angus McBride** (Linden Artists) 228–229; **David Mitcheson** 204–205; **Nicki Palin** 144–145,
148–149, 152–153, 182–185, 202, 206–207, 218–219, 232–233, 236–237, 288–289, 310–311, 314*tl*;
Maurice Pledger (Bernard Thornton Artists) 320–321; **Bryan Poole** 322–327; **Sebastian Quigley** (Linden Artists) 16–23,
26–27, 98–99; **Claudia Saraceni** 190–191; **Stephen Seymour** (Bernard Thornton Artists) 110–111*m*; **Roger Stewart** (Virgil
Pomfret Agency) 118–119; **Ian Thompson** 24–25, 28–31, 100–101; **Richard Ward** 116–117, 188–189; **Russ Watton**
(Garden Studio) 102–103, 108–109, 110*b*, 111*r*, 202*tl*, 203*ml*; **Linda Worrall** (Linden Artists) 84–85, 86*ml*, 90–91; **David
Wright** (Kathy Jakeman) 278–281, 284–285, 292, 298–299, 302–303.